W.L. "BILL" ROLLER

4.95
cl
DJE
1965 H-R
176 pgs
w/index
1st edition

THE DEMANDS OF FREEDOM

THE DEMANDS OF FREEDOM

Papers by a Christian in West Germany

HELMUT GOLLWITZER

With an Introductory Essay by

PAUL OESTREICHER

of the British Council of Churches

HARPER & ROW, PUBLISHERS

NEW YORK AND EVANSTON

Selected and translated from the German
Forderungen der Freiheit
(Chr. Kaiser Verlag, München)
by Robert W. Fenn
with additional papers

THE DEMANDS OF FREEDOM

Copyright © 1965
by SCM Press Ltd.

Printed in the United States of America. All rights reserved. No part of this book may be used or reproduced in any manner whatsoever without written permission except in the case of brief quotations embodied in critical articles and reviews. For information address Harper & Row, Publishers, Incorporated, 49 East 33rd Street, New York 16, N. Y.

FIRST EDITION

Library of Congress Catalog Card Number: 65-10370

CONTENTS

HELMUT GOLLWITZER IN THE EUROPEAN STORMS

An Introductory Essay by Paul Oestreicher

I

THEOLOGIANS don't write best-sellers. This is at least as true in Germany as in Britain where Dr Robinson's phenomenal success is surely the exception that proves the rule. Germany's exception (but not its John Robinson!) is Helmut Gollwitzer whose *Und Führen Wohin Du Nicht Willst* ran into many editions and translations[1] a decade before *Honest to God*. If I begin by mentioning this book it is not because it is the most important landmark in the author's life but because, like many others, I was initially drawn by this book into the orbit of his life and thought. Today Helmut Gollwitzer as a prophetic Christian thinker stands in a curious relationship to the book that established his popular reputation. It is a moving description of the five years (1945-50) spent in the Soviet Union as a prisoner of war. In its essence the book is a record of his own deep involvement with people, his fellow prisoners and the many Russians whom he managed to engage in dialogue. At the same time the author could not help describing Russia at the height of Stalinist tyranny. The immediacy and honesty with which this was done inevitably meant that the book would find a place in the anti-Communist literature of the cold war epoch. This undoubtedly and, as will become evident, paradoxically explains part of the book's success, particularly in West Germany where anti-communism is endemic. But to the discerning reader Gollwitzer's narration is totally unrelated

[1]*Unwilling Journey*, SCM Press, London, and Fortress Press, Philadelphia, 1953.

to cold war pamphleteering in literary guise. It is the deeply personal testimony of a man who is wholly committed to men both as individuals and in society; it is the record of one who is not only a pastor by profession but by an inherent inability to be anything else. Here was a man who honestly described the evils of communism which he encountered as a prisoner, yet one who evidently loved communists as fellow human beings and thought of them as brothers.

Helmut Gollwitzer was born in 1908, one of six children of the Lutheran pastor of a south German village. He graduated from high school in the ancient city of Augsburg. To this day a strong accent betrays his Bavarian homeland. His personality and appearance point rather to a peasant rooted in the soil than to a parson of academic distinction. It seems that in him the shrewdness of the peasant has been transmuted into the wisdom and intellectual discernment of a highly skilled theologian. The sparkle in his eyes betrays a sense of humour that he shares with few German theologians. He does share it with his much loved mentor and friend from across the Swiss border, Karl Barth. I imagine he might equally well have become a great clown or a classic 'little man' on the tragi-comic stage, not only because of his natural ability to act, but because he communicates from heart to heart as readily as from mind to mind. Indeed when he is entirely thrown back on the mind, he is as capable of falling prey to academic obscurity as any professional theologian, or at any rate as apt to fall victim to the linguistic maze of German syntax.

The German university system has produced a professorial image to which Helmut Gollwitzer does not conform. While still a prisoner in Russia the University of Bonn called him to the chair of systematic theology which Karl Barth had vacated soon after Hitler came to power. The succession in 1950, after years of heresy and terror, could not have pleased Barth more. I first met Helmut Gollwitzer five years later when I joined his faculty as a research student. Most people by now had read his book about Russia. Because of this popular success many students tended to regard his theological scholarship less highly than they would have done had he conformed to the pattern of the authoritarian and remote professor with a large number of more or less intelligible books to his credit. Yet the sources of suspicion of his scholarship went deeper than mere distrust of the popular, and for two distinct reasons.

First, Gollwitzer's determination to remain a preacher and a pastor is most unusual on the German academic scene, where devotion to pure scholarship has almost religious overtones. In a manner much more readily understood by Anglo-Saxons, Helmut Gollwitzer was a pastor to his students (and not only to his) before he was their teacher. The same, it seems, had been true of Dietrich Bonhoeffer who, unlike Gollwitzer, had been strongly influenced by Christian life outside Germany and specially in Britain. It is not the custom for the German academic teacher to be freely available to his students for advice, nor to live among them. A short *Sprechstunde* (consultation hour) once or twice weekly is the best that students can hope for. They are so much intimidated that, from my experience, this *Sprechstunde* in the case of most professors more than suffices. Not so for Helmut Gollwitzer. Whenever I tried to see him the queue was always too long and I knew that these students had not for the most part come to discuss the relative merits of Bultmann and Barth. They were more likely to have been moved by last Sunday's sermon delivered in the large overcrowded lecture hall that then still served as the university church. Or even more likely, an affair of the heart was drifting on to the rocks. How often students have no one to turn to at such moments, moments when they could not care less about the dry bones of academic theology. Ten minutes of real involvement in their problem by one who cares deeply may have taught them more applied theology than ten hours in the lecture room. And this pastoral caring finds eloquent expression in Gollwitzer's preaching which has the greatness of simplicity that his other writing sometimes lacks. Many people have learnt to be thankful for this ability to get through to them with the Word of God in a context that is at the same time universal and directly personal. It is never the conscious *ad hominem* preaching of evangelical exhortations but rather the joyful proclamation of the 'Christian Psalmist' that the God who has overcome evil is present both in judgment and in healing forgiveness. It is preaching in which love both indicts and reinstates, preaching that reaffirms the Kingdom here and now . . . the Kingdom within *you*.

Of this I can speak from deepest personal experience. My own engagement was broken off during my time in Bonn. I was profoundly distressed. I dragged myself to church that Sunday, in bitterness expecting nothing but stones. It seemed, an hour later, that I had come away not merely with bread but with the pearl of great price. Yet the preacher had known nothing of my presence, let alone of my particular need. Never since that day have I been able to scorn the word 'comfort', a word that I had often been tempted to wish away from the liturgy. I had learnt—or should have learnt—more about preaching on that occasion than in subsequent years of sermon classes. Of equal significance is that a person of little or no education would have been no less aware on that occasion than I of the presence, the power and the love of Christ. Such preaching and pastoral involvement, as I have observed, is unusual in German academic circles and casts some doubt on one's scholarship, at least among the less spiritually perceptive.

Yet Helmut Gollwitzer went on to break with tradition in an even more radical sense or, if not quite breaking it, he chose to build on a tradition that neither university nor church in Germany have been ready to adopt. He was prepared to risk his academic reputation by committing himself politically to a clearly defined set of 'anti-establishment' positions which he defended with theological zeal. Had he stopped at proclaiming the saving power of Christ for the individual, the kingdom *within*, there would have been little controversy. The *Kirchenkampf*, the struggle against heresy within the Church and against inhumanity outside it during the years of Nazi power, as well as his Soviet imprisonment, had taught him the need to preach the immediate relevance of the Kingdom to the political and economic life of man. This could still have remained ivory-tower-preaching, mere academic 'awareness' of a type fairly common in the 'life and work' theology that has become ecumenically fashionable while remaining almost deliberately ineffective. In contrast to this Helmut Gollwitzer threw himself passionately into the political conflicts of the German Church, conflicts rooted in the fundamental theological differences that disrupted German protestantism during the years of Nazi rule and continue to do so. The issues are German, the problems posed by them are universal. Helmut Gollwitzer's present response to some of these is both the subject of this book and the preoccupation of a large part of his life. It is this even more than his pastoral dedication that makes him unusual, although not unique, as a systematic theologian. What is most astonishing is that despite all this and perhaps even more because of it he has, over the last ten years, established an *academic* reputation that few would still attempt to assail. Nor has anyone dared to challenge his personal integrity.

To understand all this we must go back into the past, but before we do so, before we look at the life of this prophetic and therefore highly controversial Christian, a further aspect of his character must be mentioned: his apparently limitless charity towards his opponents. Even in the most hard-hitting personal debate, the most passionate dispute, even when maliciously slandered, he has seemingly never sought to hurt his opponent or appeared to despise him. If it seems odd to have to say this of any Christian theologian, the truth is that the sad record of post-war German ecclesiastical controversy makes it both necessary and significant.

Helmut Gollwitzer studied philosophy (Hardtmann, Heidegger) and theology in the years 1928-32. In true German fashion he went from university to university; from Munich to Erlangen, to Jena and finally to Bonn seeking out those teachers whose scholarship had most to offer him: Althaus in Erlangen, Gogarten in Jena and then Karl Barth to whom, in 1937, in Basel, he presented his doctoral thesis, a study of the eucharistic doctrine of Lutheran orthodoxy as evidenced in its conflict with early Calvinism. What is perhaps most significant in this academic progression is that it began with a study of philosophy. The significance lies in the traditional alienation between philosophy and the theologians in German protestantism, an alienation dating back to Luther's rejection of the medieval scholasticism of which he was so much the product. The result has been an almost total lack of communication between some of the most important strands of German intellectual development over a period of centuries. The dialogue with the philosophers has recently been taken up by Helmut Gollwitzer and its significance is likely to be as great for thought in Britain as in Germany. Indeed, the *Honest to God* debate is likely to reach stalemate unless our radical theologians acquire the philosophical equipment needed to make meaningful inroads on the secular categories of present day thought. This, Helmut Gollwitzer has modestly and from a relatively secure theological base begun to do. His recent book on *The Existence of God*, already reprinted in Germany, can now also be studied in English.[1]

Of the early and most fundamental theological influences on his life Gollwitzer wrote to a friend: 'The vital influences on me were those of Barth and Luther. The two converged in such a way that I find it difficult to say which was the greater or where one began and the other ended. And it is no doubt important that my theological beginnings reach back to the period when dialectical theology was displacing both theological liberalism and conservatism and when the work of Bultmann, which I took very seriously, opened our minds to the essential role in theology of the historically critical approach to biblical studies. My position somewhere between the Barthian and Lutheran fronts determined my earlier theological work on the sacraments and on the question of confessional reunion and is still the basis of my present concern with the relation between law and Gospel. It is this latter theme that has also given rise to my interest in the problems of political ethics and in a question that increasingly occupies me, the relationship be-

[1] SCM Press, London, and Westminster Press, Philadelphia, 1965.

tween the Church and the Jews (Israel). This problem I believe to be a critical theological issue today with an importance that has gone unrecognized for centuries. Personal experience, recent history and two journeys through Israel have convinced me of this, as has an active participation in ecumenical discussion for which my work on the conflicts within protestantism was a useful preparation. Only lack of time has prevented me from active involvement in the ecclesiological debates of the ecumenical movement in which I have nevertheless felt involved through close personal friendship with many of the protagonists. Similarly I have not found time to enter into the theological dialogue with Roman Catholicism that I would welcome in view of the strong impression made on me in the past both by Catholic piety and by the conversion to Catholicism of some of my friends.'

After serving a curacy in Munich and a brief period as pastor in Vienna, Helmut Gollwitzer in 1936 took up a post which committed him fully and publicly to the struggle against Hitler and more immediately against those elements in the Church which had come to terms with German fascism and the racialism that went with it. He joined the Council (*Bruderrat*) of the Confessing Church in Thuringia. In effect this meant joining the faithful remnant of the Lutheran Church in the German province that before any other had chosen Nazi rule and in which the 'established' *Landeskirche* had embraced the distorted faith of the 'German Christians' more readily than any other regional Church had done. It is not surprising that Gollwitzer had his first experience of Nazi arrest in 1937. What is more surprising is that he found time in this tragic, turbulent period to complete his doctoral thesis and to present it to Karl Barth in Basel. On his release, Gollwitzer was banned from Thuringia and began an association with Berlin that was to last until 1940 and to be resumed in 1957. At the age of 29 he took over the 'portfolio' for theological education in the Prussian Council of the Confessing Church. He also taught in that Church's illegal and therefore underground seminary in Berlin. Into this period fell the arrest of Martin Niemöller, the acknowledged leader of Christian resistance to Nazism. He was to remain a prisoner until the defeat of Nazi Germany. His release by American troops in 1945 coincided almost exactly with Helmut Gollwitzer's capture by the Red Army. Between them, they spent thirteen years behind barbed wire. Martin Niemöller at the time of his arrest was pastor of the parish of Dahlem in Berlin. Not only was this one of the wealthiest suburbs of the German capital, but in it lived a high proportion of the most influential and powerful people in Nazi Germany. To preach the Gospel here was to preach it in the open jaws of hell. But there were also courageous men and women here who were among the moral and intellectual leaders of the opposition to Hitler. In the days preceding World War II there could hardly have been a more interesting parish in all Europe in which to work—or a more dangerous one. Martin Niemöller chose Helmut Gollwitzer to fill his place. The continuity of courageous biblical (and therefore anti-Nazi) preaching was assured for as long as the Gestapo would permit, preaching firmly based on the statement of faith of the 1934 Synod of Barmen where the Confessing Church proclaimed that in all spheres of life, Jesus Christ, and he alone, was the final authority to whom allegiance was due.

Gollwitzer stayed at his post until after the outbreak of war. Some of his sermons from this grim period have been translated into English under the title *The Dying and Living Lord.*[1] In 1940 he was forbidden to preach or speak anywhere in Germany and was expelled from Berlin. Later that year he was drafted into the *Wehrmacht* and served in France in the infantry. It is hard to escape the conclusion that the concentration camp could have been the only alternative.

Into this last period of his parochial ministry falls a tragic episode in Gollwitzer's personal life, and one that must at the same time have deeply influenced his whole subsequent life, both private and public. In fact no single event could have more profoundly convinced him of the indivisibility of what is private and public, personal and political. Gollwitzer was

[1]SCM Press, London, and Fortress Press, Philadelphia, 1960.

engaged to the daughter of a famous actor. His fiancée was half Jewish. A marriage between a German and a Jew (or a 'half Jew') had, by 1940, been made illegal. Yet one of the characteristics of a totalitarian state where the law is arbitrarily created is that its provisions can as arbitrarily be waived for those with friends in the right quarters. Paradoxically Helmut Gollwitzer found such a friend in Hermann Göring's sister who, despite everything, had continued to come to his services. She managed to enlist the support of Göring's wife who had herself been an actress and who had high regard for the father of Gollwitzer's fiancée as an actor. Emmi Göring succeeded in getting permission for Fräulein Bild to marry, but when the Gestapo informed Göring *whom* she was to marry, this permission was revoked. The young pastor's fiancée thereupon took her own life. There is no better place in which to record that after his return from Russia Helmut Gollwitzer married the girl who had been his fiancée's closest friend. She too was half Jewish and had survived the Nazi holocaust. Without her help, encouragement and often protection from a much too demanding public, Helmut Gollwitzer's work today would be unthinkable.

Inevitably this heart-rending encounter with the demonic effect of anti-semitism made Helmut Gollwitzer particularly sensitive to the need for a complete reappraisal of the Christian attitude to the Jews and their reinstatement not only as individuals but as a people with an essential part to play in the *Heilsgeschichte* within which God has accorded them a special and honoured place. He is among those today who are not merely opposed to anti-semitism but who are acutely aware of the historic guilt of Christendom in preparing the ground for Auschwitz and of the guilt of the German churches—even their anti-Nazi minority—in doing too little too late to help the Jews and even then largely concentrating that help on those Jews who had become Christians. 'We have not lived our faith in relation to the Jews,' says Gollwitzer, 'and so we have lost the right to proclaim it to them. They are as much God's chosen as we. The new covenant does not annul the old.' And so he is convinced that the Jews must be included as an integral part of the ecumenical movement, a conviction shared today by those Roman Catholic theologians who have, against opposition that has yet to be overcome, included a chapter on the Jews in the Vatican Council schema on ecumenism.

To wear the uniform of Hitler's army was no easy thing for Helmut Gollwitzer. Even before the outbreak of war, on a visit to Switzerland, he had agreed in conversation with Karl Barth that a Nazi victory would be a disaster. Although not a pacifist, either then or now, it troubled him greatly that he might be called on to kill in a manifestly unjust war. In fact he managed never to fire a shot and eventually obtained a transfer to the ambulance corps as a stretcher bearer at the Russian front. At least he was engaged in healing which is a Christian's business wherever he may be, whatever the circumstances. And so to Germany's capitulation, his capture by the Red Army and imprisonment. Released on January 1st 1950 he went straight to the University of Bonn after a short period of rest. Bonn had meanwhile become the capital of the German Federal Republic.

II

Both the secular and the ecclesiastical history of post-war Germany (more accurately perhaps of the post-war separated parts of Germany?) are much too complex to outline satisfactorily in an essay such as this, yet some such attempt must be made if the role of Helmut Gollwitzer in this pattern of events is to be appreciated. When he arrived on the scene in 1950 the general situation that still obtains today had already been established; this is true of both Church and state.

In 1945 the Nazified 'German Christians' were totally and publicly discredited. The more prominent disappeared from the ecclesiastical scene altogether, others were happy to be given some minor pastoral responsibility often in some completely different regional church. The leaders of the Confessing Church were now *de facto* the leaders of German Protestantism. The provincial structure of the Church was rapidly reorganized alongside the new civil administrations and leaders elected. A central Council and Synod were established as the supreme organs of a federation of all the German ecclesiastical provinces in both East and West. By far the most significant single post-war event and one that preceded the crises and dissensions that later arose was the signing of the Stuttgart Declaration, a confession of guilt by the German church leaders for 'not having confessed with greater courage, prayed with greater faith, believed with greater joy and loved with greater zeal'.

The declaration was addressed to Christians in the ecumenical movement outside Germany. Many of those who were now asking for forgiveness with their people had themselves suffered at the hands of the Nazis. They were ready in solidarity to share the guilt. Wurm, Dibelius, Lilje, Niemöller . . . these were some of the survivors of the resistance who signed the confession, men who were now the Church's bishops and leaders. To what extent they *represented* the German clergy and laity at Stuttgart will always be open to debate. What is important and not surprising is that the majority of German clergy had never overtly joined the German Christians in apostasy or the Confessing Church in opposition. There was and will always be a way of 'faithfully' preaching the Gospel without giving offence to anyone. These are the un-political parsons who always come up smiling and are undaunted by Christ's words: 'He who is not for me is against me.'

It very soon became evident that profound theological differences had always existed within the Confessing Church. These now became evident, not so much in matters of faith and order (to use well known ecumenical categories) but of life and work. As in the past, theological differences crystallized around political issues, only now with no Hitler on the scene it was to be less easy to separate the sheep from the goats. In one sense the divisions were the universal ones between conservatives and radicals, between left and right, progressive and reactionary. Once again the majority preferred not to take sides, knowing full well that this is the least obtrusive way of remaining on the side of the established order. The status quo always depends on an uncommitted majority who want to see it maintained—by others. The new 'establishment' of West Germany is just such an order, rooted in a bourgeois pre-Nazi past, highly successful since its organized start in 1948, ruled by a conservative party calling itself the *Christian* Democratic Union. From the very start both the Protestant and the Catholic Churches were given places of honour and even of power within society. Above all they were assured of a generous share of the community's wealth. Through the good offices of the state's tax machinery at least 1 per cent of gross national income (10 per cent of all income tax plus additional grants) was to be shared out among the two churches in proportion to their membership, which is in fact roughly 50/50, with proportionately smaller sums for other recognized religious groups. West Germany sought not so much to establish *a* church but rather to establish 'Christianity' as such, to subsidize it heavily and eventually to bring about a situation akin (yet *very* different) to the American situation where the national way of life is often thought to be coextensive with Christianity. In this context the Church is not so much tied to the state (*Staatskirche*) as to the people as a sociological entity (*Volkskirche*). One of the results of this is that *formal* membership of the Church is almost an assumed part of citizenship. *Formally* to leave the Church is a legal step taken in the presence of a magistrate which, in the present climate of opinion, comes close to opting out of society. The vast (unbelieving) majority prefer to stay in *and* pay their church tax, however reluctantly. Needless to say this all applies only to West Germany. In the East the pressures are nearly all the other way.

Clearly such a church structure built into a conservative ('restorative' is the more common German term) communal framework is bound to contain its dissenters and their dissent will crystallize around certain concrete issues. In the United States the great rallying point for the dissenting Christian minority has been the question of racial equality. In Britain it has been the demand for unilateral nuclear disarmament. In Germany it has been more complex, centring around the attitude to communism and the cold war, to the two German states and the need for their reunification and closely connected with all these to the issue of rearmament. On this whole complex of questions affecting the future of Germany and the peace of the world, German protestantism has been grievously divided, at least since 1948 when both German states were established. Broadly speaking those German churchmen whose thought and faith is dictated by Lutheran orthodoxy have been staunch defenders of the western 'Constantinian' establishment. The names of Dibelius and Lilje come most readily to mind. Their following is, if only implicitly, very large.

Ranged on the other side, again broadly speaking, are those former members of the resistance whose theology stems from Karl Barth, and who learnt during the Nazi era to reject much more than just Hitlerism. They came to question the structures of the Church itself and to engage in a radical critique of society based on an existential (Bonhoeffer) or neo-orthodox (Barth) reinterpretation of the person and will of Christ. The enthronement of Christ as proclaimed at Barmen remains their sole valid criterion of judgment. Their most prominent and prophetic voice was and remains that of Martin Niemöller. Their most lucid and penetrating theological spokesman is Helmut Gollwitzer.

Much of the new *Kirchenkampf* (church struggle) has inevitably revolved around communism, not as a politically disputable theory but as a fact of power politics in Europe. To understand the emotive climate of Germany one must bear in mind that most of its traditions and illusions died with Hitler. Little that unifies was left. There did remain anti-communism. Every 'respectable' German had, since the Russian Revolution, been taught to despise bolshevism. In the bourgeois Weimar Republic such an attitude was necessary to the survival of the state. The Nazis turned it into doctrine. The communists were to die in the concentration camps before the Jews, without a murmur of Christian protest. And in the merciless war against the Soviet Union the hatred of communism was fanned into a hatred of the Russian people who were massacred with a ferocity otherwise reserved only for the Jews. All this was followed by humiliating defeat, Russian (and Polish) annexation of Germany's eastern provinces together with the brutal expulsion of their German population. Finally there followed the Stalinist 'colonization' of an embittered East Germany and its gradually enforced communization.

Little wonder that anti-communism was West Germany's most ready-to-hand rallying point. The Western allies chose to capitalize on it, to use West Germany as a powerful weapon in the cold war; more than that, to enlist her as a potential ally in any future armed conflict. To this whole development a Christian minority, politically ineffective, as it turned out, cried No. Gollwitzer was one of them and the one most universally respected. Some of that respect, to his own embarrassment, stemmed from his book on Russia. He might have written it a little differently had he anticipated the welcome it would get for reasons he could hardly applaud. But the respect he commanded and continues to command has sounder reasons. His human warmth, his lack of rancour and his candid integrity make him a difficult man to attack. Significantly a warm friendship united him with Germany's first post-war president, the late Professor Theodor Heuss, a truly liberal and deeply cultured man of letters who, although almost certainly in disagreement with much of what Gollwitzer stood for, was not above consulting him on the political (and therefore moral) questions that were dividing honest men.

The attitude to communism was vital for more than one reason. Gollwitzer, who was virtually forced into a detailed study of its doctrine by the label of 'expert' that was pinned on him, knew only too well that a fresh wave of anti-Soviet hatred could only end in disaster. Furthermore Marxism not only contained certain positive elements compatible with the Gospel, it voiced genuine grievances against the Christian Church. To enter into dialogue was the only possible way forward. No one knew better how hard it was, and how necessary.

While basic charity and the call to Christians to be reconcilers amply justifies this dialogue theologically, practical political considerations *demanded* it—so Helmut Gollwitzer and his friends argued in the face of angry opposition. Even to appear to have communist sympathies, they were quickly to learn, is the one thing for which there is no room in West German society both inside and outside the Church. It is a significant fact of post-war West Germany, but one that cannot be analysed in any detail here, that the only centre of genuinely liberal non-conformity was in the 'left wing' of the protestant church. Besides Niemöller and Gollwitzer, some other leading figures deserve mention. There was the late Professor Hans Iwand, another theologian at the University of Bonn, who was passionately devoted to building bridges of friendship to the Orthodox and protestant Christians of Eastern Europe who were being largely dismissed in the West as crypto-communists. Iwand was the prime German mover in the establishment of the Prague Christian Peace Conference which since 1958 has sought to provide on Eastern soil a genuine place of ecumenical encounter between East and West. Of this Conference and its president Josef Hromádka more must be said below.

Then there is the uniquely interesting figure of Dr Gustav Heinemann, an eminent lawyer and the first President of the Synod of the reconstituted German Church. Deeply committed to the theological insights of the Confessing Church he entered politics, and in 1948 joined Dr Adenauer's first Cabinet as Minister of the Interior. When Adenauer announced his decision to rearm West Germany Dr Heinemann resigned, the only German minister since the war to have laid down office on a point of principle. He was later to be re-elected to the Bundestag as a member of the Social Democratic opposition. Perhaps the greatest symbolic moment of his political career, apart from his resignation, came in the foreign affairs debate when Germany's integration into NATO was at issue. With the controlled passion of his legal mind he argued against the cold war concepts developed by John Foster Dulles and followed by Dr Adenauer. He was frequently heckled and interrupted from the floor of the House. Over the heckling and now with profound fervour he was heard to shout: 'Let me remind you that Jesus Christ died for Karl Marx too.' Pandemonium broke out. Millions of Germans in East and West were listening on the radio. Keir Hardie might have caused a similar scene in the House of Commons many years ago.

This pandemonium in the arena of politics evoked by a fundamental evangelical proclamation caught in a flash the essence of the division among German Christians. At that moment Gustav Heinemann was not the spokesman of a political party but of a Christian minority whom it has not been possible to silence, a minority organized today in the *Kirchliche Bruderschaften* (Church Brotherhoods), a politically conscious minority of clergy and laity who consider themselves the true heirs of the religious anti-Nazi struggle. Their leaders continue to be highly respected but not all have retained positions of authority. Martin Niemöller, now one of the six presidents of the World Council of Churches, continues to be President of the important church province of Hesse-Nassau (re-elected by a majority of one vote) but he has felt obliged to resign his seat on the Central Council of the German Church and was removed from the post of President of its Foreign Office. Gustav Heinemann is no longer President of the All-German Synod. The pendulum has swung far to the right since 1946. Yet throughout all the struggles within the ecclesiastical 'machine' those best able to maintain their independence have been the university professors of whom a small minority belong to the *Bruderschaften*, Vogel and Fischer in Berlin, Wolf in Göttingen, Steck in Frankfurt and some less well known. Two others deserve mention, the conciliatory President of the Church in Westphalia, Ernst Wilm, and finally Dr Heinz Kloppenburg, the indefatigable and jovial cigar smoking leader of the peace movement within the German Church, Chairman of the German branch of the Fellowship of Reconciliation and, together with Martin Niemöller, one of the few wholly committed to Christian pacifism. However much all these men may have in common theologically and politically, they are individualists who by no means always agree with each other. The degree and nature of their radicalism differs widely and while it is almost certain that Helmut Gollwitzer is as radical as any of them in his ultimate conclusions it is equally true that his pleading is often the more persuasive for its scholarly moderation. When it is remembered that he is a Bavarian and that the Bavarians are known as Germany's hot-heads, this is no mean achievement.

Clearly Helmut Gollwitzer has not sheltered behind his 'academic immunity'. Not only has he marshalled intellectual arguments, he has entered both the ecclesiastical and political arenas. In the All-German Synod which until the building of the Berlin Wall represented the whole German Church he has played an active role and been a persuasive advocate of unpopular causes. I was present at the Synod of 1960 held in Berlin. Gollwitzer's seat was beside that of Dr Eugen Gerstenmaier, also a theologian and the Speaker of the Bonn Parliament. Two men more similar in physical stature and more different in what they stand for would be difficult to imagine. Both of them protestant theologians, both of them involved in the opposition to Hitler (although the *nature* of Gerstenmaier's involvement in the opposition is subject to some debate), they now represent opposite poles in the Church. One is the prophetic figure almost wholly dissociated from the secular 'establishment', the other is number two in the hierarchy and known to the German public for his love of big game hunting in Africa. Yet—and it remains significant—they are prepared to sit down together in the Synod and there to speak to each other as Bruder Gollwitzer, Bruder Gerstenmaier . . . as brothers. This sort of fact is spiritually significant and may yet become politically important as the face of Europe rapidly changes.

For the German Church even more than for other Christians the Jewish question is both painful and spiritually crucial. It was debated in this 1960 Berlin Synod. Almost everything was said about anti-semitism that could be said, generalities which every Christian today must endorse; and finally a complex resolution was tabled which on closer examination said no more than that anti-semitism is a bad thing. It would obviously be passed. At a late stage Helmut Gollwitzer caught the eye of the chairman and rose to speak. 'I propose an amendment; the addition of one sentence to the resolution: *Whoever strikes a Jew, strikes the Church.*' The amendment was defeated.

Gollwitzer has gone beyond the lecture room, the pulpit and the floor of the synod. These, and particularly the first two, are for him indispensable to each other. Lecturing only makes sense to him in the living context of the preaching of the Word of God. But he has also been ready to go out into the streets and public assemblies. He has been actively involved in the German equivalent of the Campaign for Nuclear Disarmament, speaking at its Easter rallies. But unlike most of his Anglo-Saxon counterparts he has written detailed and scholarly studies on the ethics of war in the nuclear age. As a non-pacifist he is convinced that the use or even threatened use of nuclear weapons is theologically indefensible. His arguments have not been answered. Yet in Germany as elsewhere most Christians have decided to leave the issue in the hands of the politicians.

But Germany is not a place like any other. It is a nation divided between East and West. Perhaps in 1965 it can already be said: it is two nations. While Gollwitzer and his friends are anything but old style nationalists they, like all conscientious Germans, are concerned about the disunity of their homeland and about the threat this presents to the peace of the world. From the beginning, when Niemöller's voice was still the one most often heard, the protestant left were convinced that to build up Western Germany against the East within an integrated Western power-bloc would perpetuate the division of Germany and condemn East Germany to an indefinite and bleak future as a Soviet satellite and as a buffer against a re-militarized West Germany which, rightly or wrongly, Russians, Poles and Czechs would unquestionably fear. Gollwitzer and his friends tirelessly maintained that a much better hope for the peace of Europe would be a neutral, demilitarized, reunited Germany. They are convinced that at least until 1955 the Russians would have accepted such an offer and left East Germany. Indeed, the offer had been made. Whether it was sincere was never put to the test. Dr Adenauer stood for the opposite point of view. A policy of strength, he maintained, was bound to pay off. Eventually East Germany would fall like a ripe plum into the Western lap. No such thing has happened. The German fronts have hardened and this at a time when others are beginning to ask whether the cold war in Europe is not already a subject for the historians. If West Germany is allowed to have a hand on the nuclear trigger the German problem will become even more acute and the relative misery of the virtually imprisoned East Germans even more permanent. Whether the Soviet Union would still consider German reunion is an open question. A prior condition would certainly be the recognition of both German states. They might then be prepared to see one of them cease being communist if the other and more powerful ceased to appear to be a threat. The eastern fear is a vital political factor, the more understandable as West Germany has shown no readiness to recognize the eastern frontier drawn in 1945.

Clearly all these issues are political. Yet they are not in the realm where one opinion is as good as another. They intimately affect the lives of millions of people and ultimately the peace of mankind. The struggle against Nazism taught Gollwitzer and others that issues such as these inevitably raise vital spiritual questions. The confrontation with communism which is at the heart of the crisis involves not only the future role of Germany in Europe. It poses the question to the Germans whether they are genuinely prepared to break with a bedevilled past and to make friends with those peoples whom they have most severely wronged, the Jews first of all and then the Poles and Russians. Significantly in this context Germany has still to establish diplomatic relations with the state of Israel, for fear that the Arab States might then recognize the German Democratic Republic.

I have already had cause to mention the Christian Peace Conference, an organization set up by the protestant churches of Czechoslovakia in a genuine attempt by Christians in Eastern

Europe to break out of the ghetto created for them by their own governments and by the haughty aloofness of the western churches. At the heart of this movement has stood Professor Josef Hromádka who in a very real sense stands for those Christians in the East who have accepted that Christianity cannot properly be identified with the western way of life, and that it must be as ready to witness creatively in a Marxist society as in any other. In men like Gollwitzer, Hromádka has found true friends, men who understand that wherever they may be called to witness to the love of God for all men, there is a way of doing it in spiritual freedom. In the words of Josef Hromádka: 'We are as free as we have the courage to be.' It is with this freedom that Helmut Gollwitzer is concerned in the essays in this book, however diverse the particular issues under examination. For the Christian it is not so much 'freedom from ...' as an embracing of our God-given 'freedom to ...'; freedom to love, to serve, to share and if need be to suffer.

III

In 1957 Helmut Gollwitzer returned to Berlin. The Free University, built with American money in his old parish of Dahlem to 'replace' the old Humboldt University in the Eastern Sector, took the imaginative step of calling him to a newly created chair of protestant theology within the faculty of arts. There are no students of theology at the Free University. Professor Gollwitzer is therefore free to devise lectures for students of all disciplines confronting them with the spiritual issues of our time. He is concerned therefore with the whole field of modern secular thought and the Church's response to it. In a series of dialogue lectures with the agnostic professor of philosophy that is stretching over a whole semester he is at this moment publicly debating in secular terms (and in the University's largest lecture hall) the sort of issues raised in the *Honest to God* debate and by men like Werner Pelz in Britain. And all this in the context of his on-going preaching of the Word of God and lecturing in systematic theology at the Church's Berlin Seminary, the theological college at which he had taught during the days of its clandestine existence in Nazi days.

There is one final episode in Helmut Gollwitzer's life which it would be a pity to omit. It does not add to our knowledge of him. It does add to our knowledge of the Church's situation in Europe today. In 1962 Karl Barth resigned his Chair in Basel in order to devote himself wholly to the completion of his *Kirchliche Dogmatik*. The faculty nominated Helmut Gollwitzer as his successor. It was an honour he was willing to accept even at the heavy price of leaving Berlin. But the appointment to a Swiss chair is not left solely in the hands of the university. The municipality and the state are also involved. Hardly had Helmut Gollwitzer's name been proposed when an outcry was raised in the conservative Swiss press against the appointment of this 'near-communist professor'. A bitter campaign was waged, a campaign that went far beyond factual assessment of his ability. Helmut Gollwitzer was not appointed.

This is where it would seem proper to let the essays that follow speak for themselves. If some of them are already dated, their general relevance remains unaffected. The author would be the first to stress that they open rather than close the discussion. May they increase our understanding of the glorious liberty of the children of God!

I

THE DEMANDS OF FREEDOM

INTRODUCTORY

THE DEMANDS of freedom are those claims which freedom makes upon us, not our demands for freedom or for more freedom. To say that freedom makes demands upon us means something more than that our concern about freedom demands from us all those sacrifices, for example, that we read about in the newspapers of both East and West, the voluntary restriction of our personal freedom in order to make it tolerable for our fellow men, or our contribution to the defence of the freedom of the community, in order to provide the external conditions for the freedom of the individual, and so on. The title of this book points in another direction: a free man can do more than one who is not free, he can do what a captive or a slave cannot do. Freedom is thus the ability to act, and this ability makes demands. Of course the term 'freedom' as such does not indicate what I can and ought to do, but it gives an answer to the pressing question that arises as soon as we recognize what ought to be, what we should like to do, and what the occasion demands. Whatever our environment, experience makes us conscious of many kinds of limitations. We get used to accepting them, to confining our range of vision to the restricted area within our control. *Ultra posse nemo obligatur*: our duty does not extend beyond our ability to act; the less we are in a position to do, the less our responsibility. The un-free is best off. 'What could we do in the circumstances?' 'we were under orders'. That has been a most convenient excuse offered by many people with reference to the German past, and will also be the most popular and overworked excuse in the future. Because our freedom of action will always be limited, there is always good reason for acquiescence as part of the process of human maturation, but it is at the same time a great temptation as a convenient excuse for cowardice and indolence, because it prevents us from realizing and utilizing and extending the range of action open to us. We always behave with less than our actual freedom, because of our misgivings about the uncomfortable demands which our freedom makes upon us. For this reason running away from freedom is very common. If we are free, and in so far as we are free, we can be held responsible. That is true of the simplest and most obvious freedoms such as health controlling physical freedom, or the statutory regulations restricting individual liberties, or the freedom of action of governments in international affairs. None of these freedoms is unlimited, and so are none of the consequent responsibilities, but anyone who pretends that these freedoms do not exist because of their limitations, diminishes them and helps to destroy them. One part of the world may feel justified in calling itself the 'free world' because of the statutory guarantees of individual freedom in the constitution of the countries concerned, but it must keep in mind the high standard that it sets itself by the use of the term 'free', such as the implied responsibility for the other sections of mankind that do not enjoy the same freedom. In that part of the modern world that calls itself free, not only are there still here and there conditions without freedom, which make a mockery of the term 'free world', but, what is worse, there is evidence of growing resignation in face of the increasing lack of freedom, which is a subject of sociological analysis, and under the pressure of which the individual becomes discouraged and takes refuge in the garden of his private life, his pleasures and his personal religious or aesthetic emotions. To point this out is often to be immediately but unjustly charged with fanatical democratic perfectionism. Democracy will always be an imperfect and hazardous form of public polity, that can only be maintained by a continual struggle, but that does not mean that it has to be just a facade for the absence of freedom, and that it is a sign of exaggerated idealism not to accept apathetically the indications of the transformation of democracy into a democratic facade. It is vital for democracy that the signs of its falsification are not taken lightly. That is why resignation attacks its roots. Let there be no mistake about it, apathy is already widespread again amongst the younger generation.

This is further encouraged wherever decisions which should be taken responsibly are made out to be forcibly imposed by the lack of freedom of choice. Two examples can be quoted from our recent political history:

1. When the West German government began agitating for atomic weapons for the German army, they insisted that we had no choice in the matter, since this had been asked for by NATO, and we had to fulfil our obligations to our allies. It has since become quite clear that this denial of freedom of choice was used to blanket the government's own wishes and decision.

2. It is said by influential people responsible for the rearming of West Germany that because we were completely in the hands of the occupying powers we had no alternative to acceding to their demands for a military contribution to defence. Although the matters at issue were very different—in one case mass murder and the other a momentous political decision—yet the line of argument is pretty much on a level with that put forward by Hitler's henchmen during many prosecutions—the familiar plea of being under orders. It is just not true. In spite of our political weakness we were not simply acting under orders in this matter. West Germany was not in the hands of a Stalin, who only understood dictatorship. However strong the pressure from the western powers may have been, we did not act under compulsion, but as Dr Adenauer himself admits, those responsible decided on this course of action and persuaded the majority of the population to agree: so we cannot get away with the excuse of compulsion.

This kind of appeal to ostensible lack of freedom of action

does not always imply dishonesty; it is very often self-deception. It makes it easier to surrender to our own wishes and to those of others and to run away from the demands of responsible citizenship, or to make an advantageous compromise, or to play for safety by going with the swim. All the same, in countless cases it is not a question of actual lack of freedom, but the abrogation of responsibility. This is familiar in every-day life. It is characteristic of political life that it offers to anyone engaged in it the most obvious and momentous examples. The saying of Jesus that we must give account of every word we utter (Matt. 12.36) might be rephrased that we must give account of every freedom, even every minimum of freedom of action, that has been given us.

Freedom is one of the basic words of the Christian faith. The Christian Gospel proclaims freedom to anyone who takes it to heart. He is told that he is not abandoned in his weakness and solitude to the countless forces and influences of unfreedom within him and around him, but that he has a Master, Friend and Brother on his side, who is able to deal with these forces. This makes him free and gives him new power and new opportunities. He is involved in the battle between his new freedom and his old bondage, a battle with many reverses, with no end or final victory in this life, but yet a battle with always new beginnings and with a promise of victory, which makes these continual new beginnings worthwhile. One of the greatest sayings about freedom in the Christian sense is in the fifth chapter of St Paul's Epistle to the Galatians, beginning with the call: 'Stand fast in the liberty wherewith Christ hath made us free and be not entangled again with the yoke of bondage.' Here freedom is to St Paul an indispensable feature of union with Christ. This union opens up new and unprecedented possibilities, and not just religious and mystical possibilities, in the hearts and minds of men, not only a change from dread to confidence, from fear to hope, and from the consciousness of guilt to the assurance of forgiveness. In the passage quoted Paul leaves no doubt that this freedom must find outward expression. Its sphere of action is just as much between one man and another as between man and God. Freedom means liberty for the other man. As comment on the words: 'Ye have been called into liberty', Paul adds immediately: 'By love serve one another.' Thus he defines freedom by love and service, and in the following passage he mentions only outward activities in which freedom is realized. That is the reason why the Christian, while not setting external freedom above interior freedom, yet is bound to take the keenest interest in civil liberties. Since his own personal freedom does not depend on these external freedoms, which can be guaranteed by a political constitution, his responsibility and his possibility of action do not end with the effective limits of this constitution. It is indeed true of him that he is free even when in chains. Against statements in this book dealing with the Christian's responsibility for freedom and justice even under a despotism, it has been objected that under a totalitarian system no possibility of exercising influence remains. The New Testament admonitions to slaves, taken seriously, definitely contradict this. A man only becomes a puppet by degrading himself into being one. The loss of external liberties does not mean the end of everything; still less does he acquire the right to suicide or the right to such unworthy and inhuman behaviour as in despair to press the button to start a nuclear war and so to choose collective suicide, or to make propaganda for it in advance. Even though his hands are tied as far as action is concerned, he is still responsible for his words, thoughts, judgments, opinions, wishes and feelings. They too are part of his effectiveness: they too have an influence. So although the freedom of a Christian extends beyond external liberties, yet he is interested in them as the area of possibility of responsible service. It cannot be said that this perception has been a driving force in the history of the public activity of Christianity in the past, but it was nevertheless a restraining influence, checking tendencies to tyranny and preventing systems similar to the oriental despotisms from becoming permanently established in western history. The increased and still mounting possibilities of the subjection of man to man in this technical age make it necessary that the Christian should feel the responsibility of freedom more consciously, more urgently and more militantly than in the past, not only for his fellow Christians but for all men. This responsibility is based on the gift of freedom, of which the Christian Gospel speaks, and which rests on the reality of God and of his demands on men. The gift of freedom makes inescapable demands.

This book is concerned all through with the recognition of and insistence on these demands in relation to the present situation. Its underlying theme can be indicated in two observations:

1. Christians everywhere must be made to realize that something special is demanded of them, even in political life. What is demanded of them is their freedom. The serious threats to humanity and human values in the second half of the twentieth century compel the Christian to face the question of his freedom and its implications in public life. Admittedly there is no 'Christian' political programme, recognizable by its special content, and for a political party to label itself 'Christian' can only lead to continual embarrassment to Christianity, which cannot but worry the members of such a party who are genuinely Christian. However, there is no doubt that much is expected from the participation of Christians—those who heed and confess the Christian Gospel—in political life, with regard both to how they think and act. We shall rightly be judged by how far these expectations are fulfilled.

2. What has to be done today must be determined by the nature of the catastrophe that has to be prevented. After the collapse of 1945 the churches in Germany felt compelled to confess: 'That we have not confessed our faith more courageously, not prayed more faithfully, not believed more gladly and not loved more ardently', as was stated in the Stuttgart Confession of the German Evangelical Church in the Autumn of 1945. This experience of our nation must have decisive significance for us. The abhorrence of the crimes of the Hitler régime and the admission of involvement in guilt for the rise and results of this system is nothing more than paltry fellow-travellership,

non-committal following of the current fashion, the popular satisfaction of current interests, and not an indication of genuine repentance and change of heart, unless at the same time concern for the future creates a definite resolve to act today so as not to be forced to make the same confession some day over new graves and new ruins. The charge that the Church has not done enough to prevent the horrors of war is justified throughout its history since Constantine. It is less well justified in regard to the outbreak of the second World War. But if through the division of Germany a third war should break out, far worse than anything known hitherto, what remains of the Church will not be able to say to what remains of mankind in Germany and Europe that in accordance with the confession of Autumn 1945 it has done all it could to prevent this catastrophe: it will rather have to confess that far too often it has lent itself to fomenting the conflicts, supporting the cold war from a religious angle, that it did not give sufficient support to efforts to find a better way, and did not unequivocally oppose plans for mutual annihilation. That is true of both the Christian confessions in our country. I am not immediately concerned with the Catholic share of guilt, for I have enough to sweep away on my own doorstep. This guilt will be the same whether the catastrophe occurs or not, for the guilt lies in the Church not doing what is necessary and possible, guilt for which an account will in any case be demanded from the churches, their leaders, their clergy and their congregations, if not by an earthly court, then certainly before the heavenly judgment seat. A new recital of confessions will not then provide an easy way of escaping this judgment. Underlying all the sections of this book is an increasing sorrow about the deep corruption of Christianity through its tangled involvement with the state in recent years, the blindness, hardness of heart and impenitence of the official Church and the consequent spiritual dereliction.

DEFENCE AND ATOMIC WARFARE

The observant reader will notice in the following articles

that, on the one hand, concern for the defence of the state even by the use of arms is considered to be the political duty of a Christian, but that, on the other hand, the rejection of nuclear weapons and thus of all war in an atomic age is considered to be increasingly a *sine qua non* of the credibility and seriousness of the Christian message. The author admits himself that these articles show a certain development in his thought. The fact that, apart from immaterial corrections, they have been published without modification is not due to any presumptuous intention of providing evidence of the author's development, but because in this way the problems facing the theologian today, and the dilemma facing the politician, can be seen. A mere revolt against the means of mass destruction as one of the greatest blasphemies of our century, however justified this is, is by no means all that needs to be done, although every attitude is likely to prove inadequate which does not contain and maintain this revolt as a constituent and vital factor. It is making everything too easy just to declare, as was done in the 'Aid to the Question of Peace', published by the Council of the German Evangelical Church and containing some very welcome statements: 'We can today no longer support the doctrine of a just war', and then to go on in the next sentence to report that the differences of opinion in the Evangelical Church concerned only the question whether the best guarantee of peace was to be seen in 'unilateral disarmament' or in 'parity of armament'. Most of the serious opponents of nuclear weapons, however, have not by any means accepted unilateral disarmament and have thereby unjustly acquired the reputation of being unrealistic dreamers. The most important thing, as discussion on the ninth of the so-called Heidelberg Theses on nuclear war shows, was the contradiction between the rejection of the doctrine of a just war and the affirmation of parity of armaments, since the possession of arms necessarily implies their possible use in war, even with the determination to avoid this if at all possible. Anyway it is impossible to reject wholesale the doctrine of a just war, since it contains an important element of truth, that might become relevant even today in particular limited situations, where a non-atomic conflict was concerned. The traditional attitude of the principal churches with regard to military service, i.e. a qualified and limited assent, seems to offer a perfectly tenable answer (while raising all sorts of issues) to the question of the Christian's participation in the administration of the political power in the territory in which he is situated. This traditional view stands in a kind of complementary relationship to the refusal of military service by groups of Christian pacifists, since both answers are mutually exclusive, both are based on inescapable duties of a Christian in the world and exercise upon each other beneficial disquieting illumination, while neither of them regarded in isolation is able to offer a complete and satisfying answer to the total complex of the relevant questions. The change brought about by the new weapons is that a war involving their use is no longer feasible as a means of defence. It inevitably destroys what it is supposed to defend. It is sheer nonsense to attempt to justify nuclear weapons and nuclear warfare on the basis of the traditional evaluation of arms and military protection and to deny the novelty of the problem presented by this technical development in warfare. No realistic attitude to the new situation has yet been achieved in spite of years of discussion. It is being prevented by the bedevilling of the other side that is favoured equally by western anti-communism and eastern anti-capitalism and also by the playing down of the situation by powerful interests through control of means of publicity, the influence of which on votes reacts in turn on the leadership itself. To these can be added the whole chorus of theological, philosophical and political writers, who still continue to refurbish the antiquated comparison of weapon with weapon, war with war, defence with defence. They obscure the realization that the sword of Damocles hanging over the head of humanity has long since ceased to be communism or imperialism; that we can deal with all these 'isms', but we cannot deal with atomic war except by erecting barriers against it by a common effort taking priority over all other conflicts. To delay or prevent the building of these barriers, or to sabotage the necessary removal of mistrust from motives of temporary advantage or traditional interests in defence or sovereignty, is to share direct responsibility for the possibility of catastrophe, which is a crime that puts the horrors of Stalin, Hitler and Eichmann into the shade. It looks rather as if this is better understood by men like Kennedy and Khruschev than by many of our politicians and their theological supporters.

Anyone who follows discussion on these questions in Germany, and also at the moment in Switzerland, cannot avoid the depressing conclusion that the revolution in the technique of war has not really produced a corresponding revolution in thinking, and that the spectre of bolshevism—or even the wish to extract as much profit as possible from membership of the western defence community—has permanently as its counterpart the systematic minimizing of the real threat to humanity and particularly to our own nation; and that through this 'self imprisonment'[1] of public opinion we are sliding nearer and nearer to the abyss. In February 1962 the West German government began its answer to the soviet memorandum of December 1961 with the statement that the outbreak of a nuclear war in Europe would not only be 'an unthinkable catastrophe for humanity' but that 'the German people could hardly survive such a war'. Thus it is officially confirmed on government authority that the emergency of defence is identical with annihilation. So wherever the word 'defence' is used in reference to the emergency in Central Europe, let the word 'destruction' be substituted from now on, in order to avoid any self-deception. Defence means destruction. What the film *Die Brücke* ('The Bridge') so movingly described on the last day of the last war is at the same time an exact description of what would happen on the first day of any new war. All the killing on the very first day will be just as senseless as on that last day. The incontestable statement of the West German government provides a yardstick by which not only its own

[1]Nikolaus Koch, *Osterrede über Ende und Anfang deutscher Politik*, 1962.

politics must be measured, but equally the attitude of mind of the whole nation. But a Church that knows the purpose of its existence, and Christians who deserve the name even in part, must be in the van of the revolution in thinking necessary to meet such a situation. Here the question at issue for the Church is no less than the meaning of her Gospel for life. This meaning is expressed in God's commands. If the Church seeks the guidance of God's commands in relation to indiscriminate and still unimaginable mass murder that goes by the name of nuclear war, then there is no doubt that God's commands and every page of the New Testament and the name of Jesus Christ stand between us and participation in such mass murder. Here it must be made clear that this is not a question of directives issued by the Church, which can therefore be withdrawn, but the guidance of the direct commands of God, which proceeds inevitably from the heart of its Gospel, from belief in the triune and living God. The question of nuclear weapons drives us to spell out afresh the ABC of the Christian faith. It reveals inescapably in the centre of the Church itself the very atheism which leading churchmen are continually warning us is too lightly tolerated by other people, and it becomes evident that within the Church a great deal of intelligence and theology has been devoted to trying to avoid the consequences of knowledge that cannot be denied. Unfortunately this has met with considerable success in the churches. It is difficult to imagine a baser sabotage of the Church's own preaching about the importance and benefit of seeking the will of God and the reward of relying on his help, than for the Church to hesitate in its duty of proclaiming the will of God in a situation so unmistakably plain and of such universal importance as the mutual international threat of blasphemous mass murder, or to manipulate that proclamation from fear of losing the comforting protection of atomic weapons.

At the beginning of an important discussion of this subject in Synod a few years ago a well known church leader took up a disastrous position by declaring that the Church must not pronounce a definite 'No' unless at the same time it can tell the responsible politicians how they can carry out this policy in political action. This showed that he was treating the 'No' like a decree of the leaders of the Church, which could not of course be issued by them if they could not at the same time show how it was to be implemented. He was acting as if the Church had to obey God's will only as they thought fit, as if the precepts of the Gospel were a matter of permission or prohibition by the Church, which can be decided or waived by the Church according to expediency and estimated practicability. The real question of seeking the will of God was thus successfully sabotaged, and playing politics substituted for it. Evidence of this is the way in which the question of atomic weapons is widely and unblushingly stated within the Church to be a political problem that has nothing to do with the core of the Gospel of reconciliation. This is acting as if the Church had a free choice whether it should speak or what it should say—but it has no such choice.

The Church has to proclaim the will of God, as made known in the biblical message, in relation to the actual situation existing at a particular time. Thus today it has to state clearly that a nuclear war is incompatible with faith in and obedience to the living God. It has not got to wait to say *that* until it has found a practical method of implementing this fact politically in the atomic age. It will certainly not be able to ignore this political question, and will participate in all kinds of discussions of it, as is being done in many places today, but these discussions lack basis and direction, if they are not preceded by the clear statement which is fundamental to the whole problem. The special and primary task of the Church is not in these discussions, but in the clear characterization of this nuclear war threatening East and West as an act of sin, despair, faithlessness and disobedience, which it warns everyone not to take part in. To shout this 'No' in the ears of politicians and peoples in the name of God is not, as church leaders often fear, to place on the responsible politicians a burden that they should not be called upon to bear: it rather helps them to recognize the burden that is placed upon them anyway in an atomic age, and to avoid any playing down or obscuring of this responsibility. It makes it clear that even to adopt nuclear weapons as a preparation against some possible evil enterprise creates a situation to overcome which is the first task of present day politics. It makes it clear that there is no evil which can be prevented by a nuclear war, which thereby becomes justifiable. In this way the Church helps the politicians to resist the temptation to consider the possible use of nuclear war against all common sense and the command of God, and to assume that nuclear armament is to be accepted as an inevitable concomitant of the atomic age.

This also means making a decision in the dilemma arising from the certainty that nuclear war is no longer a practical means of policy, while at the same time atomic weapons seem still to be a practical and irreplaceable deterrent. The Christian in political responsibility, who does not regard the commands of God as a burdensome restriction of human freedom, but recognizes them as the liberation of intelligence for meaningful action, will not be deceived by this. The balance of fear is never a stable equilibrium, presumably not even when competition in invention at last provides both sides with the ideal deterrent. So far it has been a means of preventing war, but not by any means a way of assuring peace. The fact that spokesmen in the Church also maintain it to be so betrays not only the thoughtlessness with which political propaganda is repeated, but indicates also that the statement rejecting nuclear war and recognizing that the doctrine of a just war is not applicable to it is not really to be taken seriously, and that in any case its implications have not been worked out. For the deterrent is effective only when the possibility of a military emergency is seriously reckoned with. The Christian in political responsibility who takes seriously the recognition of the wickedness of nuclear warfare, will therefore keep clearly in sight the dangers of the deterrent phase, and will regard this phase—whatever others consider its purpose to be—only as a transitional phase to be got through as quickly as possible: he will only use the presence of this armament to achieve agreement and settlement by which it will ultimately be completely eliminated. He will therefore resist the spread of this armament to other states and support every step towards its limitation, and he will be glad that with him the Church by its uncompromising 'No' is keeping awake the consciousness of the necessity for its abolition. That he does not feel this to be an onerous hindrance to his political actions will be the test whether his actions have the right objective, and that he hopes for nothing positive from nuclear weapons, but only their restriction and abolition, so removing the threat of war generally, which in our technical stage of development cannot be brought back again to the threat of conventional war. As a guiding principle a sentence of Reinhold Schneider may be quoted: 'As soon as I begin to hope for anything from modern weapons, even from the threat they represent, I am consenting to them, and am at least inclined to agree to their use in certain circumstances. I therefore share the guilt for everything that those weapons may produce, a still unimaginable sin.'

It can be said with thankfulness that some official statements from church quarters also tend in this direction. I am thinking particularly of the ecumenical movement and also of certain statements by the Pope. What has come from official Christian sources in Germany so far has been without exception either half-hearted or inadequate. Exhortations to politicians to reduce the danger of war are no substitute for the proclamation enjoined on the Church and the consequent declaration that the Church cannot but demand of its members and of all men everywhere not to take any part in a nuclear war. There is no sign either that the clergy and the churches have really accepted those ecumenical declarations or that their minds are in tune with them. The leading councils of the churches, both Catholic and Protestant, have done little or nothing here in Germany to spread this knowledge among the congregations and to bring it to the attention of the clergy. They have been much rather content that the excitement about the problem of nuclear weapons, which was not stirred up by them anyway, has died down in the churches as it has amongst the public. In three successive numbers of a local parish magazine I counted twenty-one columns devoted to the question whether the title *Kirchenrat* is desirable or not. The question of nuclear arms has never received any comparable interest in this magazine. But as long as such indifference prevails at this lower and broader level of clergy and congregations, the ecumenical declarations will remain in the air and serve no more useful purpose than a hypocritical alibi: the Church has not remained silent; it has even said everything necessary and so has nothing to reproach itself with!

The most obvious, popular and at the same time repugnant grounds for this dual attitude to a question in which there should be no hesitation for Christians, is in the assertion that we have to choose between nuclear death and spiritual death, between 'Kremlin and crematorium', as the Catholic theologian Karl Thieme expressed it so horribly in a book that attempts to show history as determined by the first coming of Christ and his approaching return. Then just at the point where it has to be made clear that the question at issue in the modern situation is to take seriously the rule of God directing history in spite of all resistance to his purpose, all this is forgotten and the author in shameful evasion talks about atomic death and the crematorium, whereas the matter at issue is not our own murder, nor the preservation of men from the perversion of the mind, but the annihilation of incalculable masses of people who are not consulted, and whose minds and bodies alike will be murdered. Such words, which unfortunately can be matched with others from other authors, reveal within a pious context all the godlessness, the naked lack of faith, which appears in the hearts of many Christians when they look at the spectre of bolshevism. Everything that is preached so beautifully at other times about the power and rule of God, the confidence of faith and the importance of prayer is suddenly forgotten, but to communists and atheists a further proof is given that it is useless to take the message of Christians more seriously than they do themselves.

This does not mean that communism, as it has manifested

itself in its history up till now, is a harmless creed, nor that in my opinion we have to surrender to it. Resistance to foreign aggression is always a legitimate task of state power. The aim of political endeavour will have to be directed particularly to removing and avoiding the alternatives 'red or dead', or more exactly 'red or the destruction of humanity', but the Church has always recognized that political conflicts are only limited conflicts, and that political resistance, which Christian tradition admitted included even the means of waging war, can only be a limited defence: it has its limitations in the forbidding of suicide and in the acceptance of those moral principles which are subsumed in the theory of the just war, and include the point of view often put forward by Pope Pius XII of the balancing of evils. This can be understood in practice as the readiness to accept injustice to oneself and even slavery, if this can only be avoided by doing violence to God's creation and the annihilation of innocent non-combatants. Anyone who disregards this limitation betrays by his action godless fanaticism and lack of faith, both in regard to the gracious guidance and universal rule of God and also in regard to the conquering power of the Gospel. The terrifying thing about these modern statements is that in the name of Christianity they abrogate this limitation, which is based on the heart of the Christian faith, and that they wipe out the example of the early Christians that is usually extolled in teaching and preaching, and that by their pessimism they take away all hope from those Christians also, who are already living within the communist sphere of power, and that they transform faith into fanaticism and so spread fanaticism among the nations. Christendom can only avoid this horrible distortion of the Christian faith, which turns the Gospel into a stimulus of hate instead of a message of peace, by renouncing at last the belief in power, which has overshadowed its history for centuries, and by seeking for itself and for its faith no kind of protection by arms, least of all by nuclear weapons. That is the demand made on Christians by the freedom given to them in Christ. With it Christianity becomes free to take an intelligent view of the world situation, which for a long time has not actually been determined by the one conflict between the communist and non-communist worlds. It becomes free to look at the whole picture and so to see this conflict as a brawl between two men in a dilapidated house, and to realize that something must be done to prevent the house from collapsing because of their quarrel and burying them both together with all the other inhabitants.

THE CHURCH IN THE GERMAN SITUATION

There is hardly any part of Christendom that could be said to have more cause than the Christian churches in Germany to ask themselves these questions and to recognize the direct line connecting their own life of worship, their prayers, doctrines and conduct with the question of international reconciliation, peace and war. They have been through the discipline of a period in which they could learn to be aware of the temptations of power politics, but they have also acquired confidence in the familiar belief that 'it is better to trust in the Lord than to put confidence in man' (Ps. 118.8). Now their task is to put what they have learned into effect in a nation which through its external collapse has at least begun to understand its internal breakdown. This nation in its western section, which had an incomparably greater freedom of choice than the eastern part, has allowed itself to be led along the path of participation in the western military alliance, which has quickly proved profitable. In the process remembrance of the horrors and the overwhelming guilt caused by the former policy of rearmament have faded more and more into the background. The occupying powers, now became allies, worked hand in hand with our own government to make sure that the people of West Germany, enjoying the benefits of the western alliance, readily allowed themselves to be deceived about the irreconcilable contradiction between integration with the West and the reunification of their divided fatherland, and about the consequent inevitable integration of the other part with the East. They consoled themselves most conveniently by abandoning their own duty of pursuing a policy of reunification in favour of making demands from the Western powers, their new allies (who could only have a slight interest or no interest at all in reunification) and similar demands from their eastern opponents. They set up the right of self-determination as a moral demand and imagined that was politics! But moral postulates are not politics, unless they are accompanied by practical measures and plans likely to attract the support of the other interested states. Not only has nothing of the kind happened, but the idea of self-determination is now extended by us to include the lost eastern provinces for which German sovereignty is claimed more and more loudly, instead of our putting forward the concept of the right of domicile, which would be confined to the return of individual refugees. In agreement with the majority of official West German opinion a Committee of the West German Protestant Church concerned with eastern policy recently protested against the view put forward by eight protestant leaders in a memorandum that had received nation-wide publicity and that stated: 'that we must abandon any claim to sovereignty over the territory lying to the East of the Oder-Neisse line' with the words: 'Anyone who advocates the right of self-determination must likewise accept moral and political responsibility for it. In the spirit of this responsibility German policy must not legalize by renunciation of rights the arbitrary dismemberment of a homogeneous national territory, or the expulsion of whole populations from their ancient homeland.'

This statement from representatives of the Church indicates incurable rigidity of mind about which the Church has a special pastoral task. It must devote itself to softening this rigid reaction against the injustice of the expulsion of a large part of our nation from its homeland. The softening of this rigidity is necessary for the sake of embittered individuals as well as for the sake of peace and the real interests of Germany. However, for that the Churches need a policy which not only does not support the prevailing official mendacity on this question, but has the courage to help the exiles to recognize the real situation and to become reconciled to it in their hearts. Nothing can alter the fact that the eastern provinces are lost for good. The expulsion of the East Germans was one of the many major crimes of this century, and it is in no way justified by the earlier German crimes of which it was the consequence, but there is no power in the world that could or would reverse the process, and every passing year establishes the existing situation more and more firmly. It is childish to refuse to recognize this painful situation, or to attack those who state the facts. It is not a question of renouncing something that we possess, but of accepting a loss that cannot be regained, and on the basis of that admission striving for a realistic policy, which seeks an understanding with our eastern neighbours and for the sake of peace lets bygones be bygones in the face of an evil past full of guilt on both sides. Such an understanding is the essential prerequisite for the reunification of our nation. To extend the right of self-determination to the eastern provinces is to sabotage reunification and to ensure that we forfeit it irrevocably. These statements are accepted as obvious political truths outside the West German Republic no less than in the East, but in our country an atmosphere has gradually developed which can only be compared with that in the Arabian states : just as nobody there who values his life dares to express aloud the sensible demand for an agreement with the firmly established state of Israel, which is in the interests of the states themselves, so in our country no politician who values his political career dares to express these incontrovertible views. By this no harm is done to anyone, only to German politics, which is so hamstrung that it is forced to substitute unrealistic declarations for political action.

It is clear from these examples how important the general climate of public discussion within a nation is for the pastoral work of the Church, with its responsibilities always extending into the political sphere. In any discussion nowadays on the question of the Oder-Neisse line, or about the prevention of further and rapidly growing estrangement and the incitement to hostility between the two parts of the German nation, and even about the still pertinent questions implied in socialism, the Germans come up against taboos that are buttressed by prohibitions, risks and denunciations. The general alignment of the press and the accommodation of the parliamentary opposition to the government line, have narrowed down the area of discussion much further still. Almost every day furnishes new evidence that our democracy will not in the long run survive the cold war between East and West and the additional cold civil war between the two parts of divided Germany. Our institutions are, to be sure, still liberal, but the people are day by day becoming less so, and in the end the institutions also are likely to follow the same trend.

In this situation it is of the greatest importance whether or not the Church resists such a decline. By 'Church' no dogmatic idea nor legal institution is intended, but the people who support the institution and are included in its framework: the congregations who unite in worship, the clergy and the officials. It will be important for the future course of events how far they as Christians are independent of the dictation of public convention, free to develop an independent point of view and to act accordingly. There were some stirrings of this freedom after the great catastrophe of 1933 to 1945. There was readiness for unsparing self-criticism and a vivid consciousness of the task of future German politics in building peace. Here the Church realized its share of responsibility, since it was pledged to the service of the spirit which was the prerequisite of such a policy. If this is replaced by the monotony of demands on others, then that is the direct concern of the mission of the Church within the nation, for in this way a mentality is encouraged again in which the German seeks to place all the blame for his misfortune, for the impossibility of regaining the lost territories or achieving reunification, on someone else—an attitude of accusation against the wicked world, which has been and can be again the germ of hatred and readiness for war. The ministry of the Church cannot combat this mentality without raising the question of the contribution made by our own policy to the present situation and so to the non-fulfilment of national claims.

A Church which has boasted till now of being the only remaining connecting link holding the German people together across the gulf of division can even less evade this responsibility. This national function did not set the Church a task alien to its nature. For here it had to validate to the governments on both sides its ministry, including its political ministry, its power for peace and its ability to follow actively the guidance of God in history. The division of our nation into two opposing blocs and social systems gave the Church the possibility of sharing the road to a new world with the Church living in a communist society, gathering new experience along this road, and also of helping the churches in the eastern system in their trials and dangers. For this, of course, considerable freedom from emotional prejudice is needed, a readiness for contrite understanding of the present difficulties, the recognition of the restrictions imposed on and accusations hurled against the Christian faith as the consequence of the Church's own guilt and shortcomings and thus as the merciful judgment of God. It means shedding all sorts of traditional attachments and observances, which are now clearly overdue for revision. It means striving for internal and external independence against attempts at absorption on the part of both political camps, and for an attitude above parties, which makes it possible to meet political leaders of both sides critically and in a spirit of reconciliation. It means thinking out afresh and more exactly the conflicts, the tasks and the Church's own attitude, and above all it means a faith freeing it from all bitterness in the invincible Gospel of salvation for all men, which we are permitted to serve. These requisites are easily enumerated, but for us limited and conditioned men so difficult to carry out that they cannot even be mentioned without prayer for the help of him who has laid this task upon us. But by keeping them in mind we are less liable to make facile judgments and to level moral accusations. We are thankful for any sign that along the path imposed by this task a few words have been spoken, a few steps taken, a few blessings received.

This great task demands that the mind of the Church should reach out beyond the mind of the nation. Only so can Christians be a 'creative minority', to use a phrase with which Hanns Lilje once so aptly described their mission. During the years following 1933 there were some signs of this, as also in the years immediately after 1945. Today it is doubtful whether the political horizon of those connected with the life of the Church is any different from that of the average citizen of the Federal Republic. Anyway the official religious press, in so far as any political views find expression in it at all, is just an echo of the secular press. The idea that Christians within a nation in such a situation have a special task, which extends even to critical examination of the politician's job, is indeed sometimes suggested in theory, but never really given practical expression. 'Disturbers of the peace' and activities that seem likely to cause disquiet about the situation receive scant sympathy. At the synods any suggestion of discussion of such subjects comes only from such disturbers of the peace and are regarded as tediously holding up the 'real business' of the Church. They support the usual apportionment of blame: terrorism is a characteristic of communism. They disregard the same terrorism on the part of the anti-communist governments in South Korea, Formosa and South Vietnam, and the conditions in the Spanish prisons. Hungary is regarded as proof of soviet imperialism; they take little notice that France fought for Algeria with much more brutal methods and with much greater loss of life among the Algerians. They do not notice that the American aims and activities against Cuba afford a precise parallel with the soviet treatment of Hungary, nor does it seem to occur to them, remembering the words of Jesus about the mote and the beam (Matt. 7.1-5), that these western examples are a greater shame to the non-atheistic states and must be a greater grief to Christians, than the crimes of the atheistic state. So their only reaction to the Berlin wall was to hurl denunciations of communist inhumanity, while successfully avoiding reference to any penitence on their own part, which this phenomenon inevitably demanded, and they seemed surprised when, for example, at the World Council of Churches in New Delhi a chilly reception was accorded to their propaganda leaflets, which contained only accusations without a trace of any mood of penitence. They emphatically reject the clumsy attempts of the communists to use biblical texts and church pronouncements for their own propaganda, but they are not at all alarmed that in the West still greater misuse of Christianity is made daily and openly and as a matter of course.

The 13th of August 1961, the night in which the Berlin wall was built, although long dreaded, burst like an unexpected misfortune and was inevitably a day of shock, hesitation and reconsideration both for the Church and for the whole nation. Some sense of shock might have penetrated our padding of prosperity into our hearts and minds about the condition of our nation, in which the young are now exhorted and trained by the leaders on both sides not to have any scruples if one day they are ordered to shoot at each other. To that end psychological training has been applied by both armies even in manoeuvres. At a South German air base of the General Defence a young officer was asked recently by visitors whether he would obey an American order to drop an atomic bomb on Dresden. Without hesitation he replied: 'Of course'. That is where we have got to, that is the real wall, that is the future of the young men when they have grown away from confirmation class and youth clubs. Is there any sign in the pronouncements and ministry of the Church of any awareness of the real background against which they are working?

It is much more convenient to place all the blame on the communists who built the Wall and to appeal to the world conscience about this inhuman act. The same world conscience remained quite unmoved by similar and severer measures, e.g. in Algeria and Angola. They forget that it was in fact surprising that this Wall, in line with other forms of communist segregation, had not been built much earlier and that the agreement about the division of Germany, which is now pathetically refused as a possible compromise about the removal of the Wall, was in reality already signed in the Paris agreements in 1955. One of the people responsible for this signature in 1955 told me in 1960 that at the time he had reckoned as a probable consequence that one day the two German armies would oppose each other with atomic weapons in civil war. As his intelligence is beyond question he must also have reckoned on the present Wall between the two sections of the nation. This Wall was therefore reckoned on and allowed for: both sides have been busy building it for ten years and the indignation about it is only an attempt at diversion. At the beginning of the Berlin crisis, leaders of the Protestant Church in Bonn pointed out that it must also be the task of West German politics to do everything possible to see that the East German government did not feel obliged to set up the state boundary at the Brandenburg Gate. What was in fact done was once again to proclaim demands on the other side, which did nothing to prevent this disaster. So the path followed by our nation goes from one disaster to another, because it goes from one failure to another. The excuse that no other course was ever possible is of course useful to ensure sleep at night undisturbed by twinges of conscience, but it works astonishingly successfully. There must be some amongst us who refuse to be lulled by it, and so at least in the Church the factual separation of the Protestant Church in Germany since August 13th 1961, the duration of which cannot be known, must be regarded as a judgment showing us that our efforts have not been free and energetic enough and not sufficiently rooted in the faith, and that we have all lagged far behind our mission. 'Thou mayest be no longer steward' (Luke 16.2). You cannot from now on be a connecting link—that is what is being said to us now, and only when we hear and ponder what is being said to us and consider how far we have given cause for it, shall we be able to take up afresh and with renewed hope our mission as a Church in the divided nation and in the divided world.

The objection is to be expected that in all this the Church is being much too closely involved in political events and so tempted to 'dabble in politics', against which the distinction made by the reformers between the mission of the Church and the function of the state is a justified warning. In the essays collected here it is hoped that the endeavour will be recognized in the light of this distinction of the reformers and on the basis of this distinction, to clarify the Church's political responsibility and at the same time to resist the temptation to make the Church a political organization. But a political ethic derived from theological insights is in the opinion of the writer only half achieved as long as nothing more is done than to draw up a few general principles governing the political service of the Church and the political responsibility of Christians. As it would be self-deception for a theologian to think that by keeping to the timeless-theoretical he would be free from the influence of his social and political environment, he is forced to attempt to understand and evaluate the actual world around him and to consider the practical relation to this world of the Christian message. Through his social-ethical work he has neither to turn the Church into the tutor of the politician nor to confine it to 'purely church affairs' and a 'purely religious' attitude, which would in fact be a pseudo-religious attitude, as long as it resulted in a denial of the world responsibility of the Church and the Christian. Hence thinking out the political situation and the social consequences of the Christian proclamation at a particular time and in particular circumstances is always the duty, not only of the social and moral philosopher, but of every theologian. One of the disappointments about German theology is that the experiences of the years 1933-45 were not enough to prevent theologians from withdrawing into a theological ivory tower, in which the theological study remains unaffected by the human conflicts all around them. One can read edifying theological treatises arguing that the belief in the resurrection interpreted existentially is faith in the death-conquering power of love, and that the *theologia crucis*, the acceptance of the cross, is the vital decision of faith, but by no means all the authors of such articles draw the consequences for their own attitude in say, the question of nuclear weapons and the work for peace.

Although the Church has neither to act as tutor to the politicians nor, from superior but amateur knowledge, to provide them with recipes for the solution of political problems that does not mean that it must content itself with general, and thus necessarily vague, principles and 'hold back', as is often said, from actual concrete questions. It will, of course, keep out of the daily political squabbles, involving assent to or dissent from particular positions, but it will not be able to 'hold back' from standing up for the victims of political decisions, from protest against terrorism and against wanton acceptance of the sacrifice of human beings. It will not be able to 'hold back' from objectively drawing the attention of those politically responsible to the urgent tasks arising from the actual situation and the responsibility for the people entrusted to them. When it seems clear that ideology or some fixed idea is tempting the political leaders to neglect their responsibility for the people and nation entrusted to them, the Church will have to protest passionately in public and in private; it will examine all the projects and show up those means and methods forbidden by the gracious will of God to men, which it is the duty of the Church to proclaim in the Gospel, and it must consequently reject as a crime the attempt often made by many of its own members to persuade it that, for example, the question of nuclear weapons is a purely political and military problem, in which the Church should not become involved. And with regard to means and methods, which in view of the difficult problems of an actual political situation cannot be condemned outright from the start, it will insist that among them there are some which can only be regarded as a last resort, but can be condemned if used at an earlier stage, while other possibilities are still open.

This last was the justified intention of the old doctrine of a 'just war', but it is valid not only in the case of war, but also in relation to the policy adopted by our government of bringing the Federal forces into the scheme of nuclear deterrence. This should have been stated with the utmost vigour by the Church, not only, but primarily, by the Christian Church in Germany, when in the unhappy and surely false opinion that it was impossible to check the dreaded soviet expansion in Europe without West German troops, it was decided to arm one half of this divided and in so many ways guilty nation. The result was to bring about the absorption of the two parts into the opposing military blocs and to make permanent the division of Germany and with it of Europe, to abandon the eastern part of the nation to communism, from which however the rest of the world was to be protected, to impede the process of change of heart and the political rebirth of this nation and to complicate the European problems to the point of insolubility. In the recent history of the German Church two instances particularly may be mentioned when such an attempt was made in the form of public declarations within these limits to make the legitimate voice of the Church heard in regard to political decisions. The first was the so-called Düsseldorf declaration in the autumn of 1954, in which influential Protestant leaders and theologians asked pertinent questions about the proposed rearmament of West Germany; the other was the so-called emergency statement of the synod of the Protestant Church of the Union in the autumn of 1957. In comparison with other church statements these two went furthest in reference to the political set-up, but kept within the legitimate range of church action. Nevertheless their sponsors yielded not only to the refusal of the government to listen, but also the verdict of a large part of church publications and press supporting this refusal theologically as being an illegitimate interference in politics. Many other attempts, for example the church deputation to the Federal government in the Spring of 1958 concerning the intention to have nuclear weapons, petered out so feebly in preliminary discussions obviously not taken seriously by the spokesmen of either side, that they are not worth mentioning. This miserable failure is only explicable by an unconfessed attachment to a political programme, that the Church should have made it its business to challenge seriously in such a critical situation. This covert attachment prevented the leaders and synods of the Protestant Church from standing by their own words with the seriousness they deserve and with which the Church would wish its words to be received. It is only necessary to recall how modestly and faintheartedly the Church stood by its pledge, given at the Synod at Weissensee in 1950, to stand up for conscientious objectors, because of legislative and administrative difficulties. That is its share of the blame resting on Christians in the German Democratic Republic for the resulting persecution. The statement once so solemnly made that a situation must never be allowed to develop in which Germans would shoot at Germans did not impel any church organization to protest when the Federal President Lübke ten years later exhorted young soldiers in the Federal army to be prepared to do just that: this exhortation is now repeated daily in the newspapers of the German Democratic Republic and the Church there can no longer cite in protest any similar protest in the Federal Republic. A third example among many: in July 1956 an extraordinary synod of the German Protestant Church passed a resolution advocating among other things an amnesty for political prisoners in both parts of Germany as a means of lessening tension. A short time afterwards the same question of amnesty was raised in the Federal Parliament and the then Minister for the Interior, Schröder, described all those who advocated the amnesty as communist agents working under the direction of a foreign power. As though the Synod in full responsibility had never supported the idea, there was complete silence in church circles, and to this day the subject has never been mentioned again, although the position in regard to political legal procedure in the East German Republic has not improved and in the Federal Republic has definitely deteriorated, so that there would be more reason than ever for the Church to enter the lists. But for that it must be free; it must not consider expediency; it must not covertly involve itself in party politics, nor must it comfort itself with pious declarations to cover the nakedness of its inactivity, but it must jump into the breach just where its proper place undeniably is in this divided world.

All that has just been set down in description of the present German situation is the direct concern of the Church in this nation. For it faces the Church with questions about whether it should speak and what it should say and do. A church which had to suffer the profound experience of the years of struggle with the Nazi régime must, one would think, be alive to such questions as: what is the significance of its presence, its worship, its organization in churches, in a nation that a short time after the greatest defeat in its history is building up again within its larger section a strong military force with which to continue the conflict with the eastern nations, which it invaded centuries ago? To what extent does the thinking in our churches about the Russians, the communists and the eastern states differ from that current in the nation generally? How far is it a matter of concern to our churches and their ministers to support a policy of peaceful reconciliation in relation to our western neighbours—an important but unfortunately one-sided element of Federal German policy! How far are our churches and their ministers concerned that every effort is being made by our government to ensure that our people should not realize the real meaning of a new European war, and in particular of a nuclear war? To what extent is there any appeal to the responsibility of the Christian churches for peace? How far are they alive to the question as to what contribution our nation can make to the reduction of tension and the removal of the danger of a nuclear war? What sort of influence do they exert on the refugees? How far are these being helped by the Church to face reality and to accept a policy of reconciliation with the eastern nations on the basis of this realization? Is the Church tackling these questions, which are also immediate pastoral problems, courageously and without any eye on popularity? Are the churches cells of freedom, in which discussion can be frank and friendly, and are they consequently alive to any limitations of freedom in the state, and are they centres of independent thought? Are they also alive to what is going on, what questions arise and what developments are taking place among their brother churches behind the iron curtain and the Wall, and are they in this way working against the growing estrangement between East and West, not by imposing the condition that Christians over there must act according to our wishes, but by taking an interest in just those differences in behaviour between eastern Christians and our own ideas? Is the fellowship of faith true of them and—to mention only one thing—does the communion of the Lord's Supper, about which they sing 'Those who eat of one Lord's body share a joint responsibility' really extend beyond all frontiers and walls? Is the idea therefore intolerable that the danger from weapons of mass destruction threatens the communicant congregations over there with annihilation to protect those on this side? Because of their common membership of one holy Church amongst all nations is it not impossible for them to take any other attitude to the reality of modern war than clearly to refuse to take part in it? Is it possible in the Lutheran Church to accept a doctrine of the Lord's Supper involving a real corporeal relation between the Lord and his disciples, and at the same time to be indifferent to a murderous attack on this created body implied by even the manufacture and testing of nuclear weapons? Does not the claim that the Lord's Supper is 'the penetration of the Spirit of Christ into our physical being', part of the 'all-embracing breaking-in of the power of God into this temporal world' become just an edifying phrase as long as it does not result in a definite 'No' to modern war? Does it make sense that in particular the Lutheran Church leaders, theologians and periodicals, which fight relentlessly for their own particular understanding of the sacraments, should not be found in the front rank of work for peace and the fight against nuclear weapons, but are instead for the most part using much theological argument to defend the other side? And again, what kind of education of the nation's opinion and will is being attempted by the Christian churches, their ministers, leaders, synods, periodicals and theological colleges, in order that real lessons may be learned from the past, and a profound re-thinking make our people determined that such a course of action is not going to be repeated?

This incomplete catalogue of questions is not a series of accusations in interrogative form. Thank God these questions cannot be answered with a flat negative. But neither can they be answered predominantly in the affirmative. They are drawn up so that we shall have them before our eyes and can test ourselves by them, and can be reminded that our worship, theology, religious teaching and our prayers are inseparably bound up with the fate of the world, as it is being worked out in political action, and with the ethics of this action. We can forget this fact, dispute it or ignore it, but we should have to cease to exist as a Christian Church if we tried to deny that in politics also special things are expected from those who are 'instructed in the way of the Lord' (Acts 18.25). The demands of freedom, the implications of the Gospel, involve political life, and this is not a matter of trivialities outside the 'real business of the Church'.

In this catalogue of questions, too, the problem of nuclear weapons, with its related political problems, is given prominence with some partiality. It is much the same in the other essays published here. The reason for this partiality is partly that these essays are 'occasional' addresses and not a systematically planned treatise, and also that the author in fact considers the political questions concerned as test questions, which reveal how far the Church and its members recognize their world responsibility and appreciate the special nature of the contribution to public events that is expected of them as Christians. The fact that economic and social problems, which are no less a part of political ethics than the political ones, are not dealt with here does not therefore mean that they are regarded as less important or that their close connection with political decisions is not recognized. The author is well aware that the destruction of our society is not threatened by nuclear war alone. G. Kennan in a seminar discussion some time ago (1961) reminded his hearers of the many other possibilities in which mankind can still make our planet uninhabitable for future generations, even if it succeeds in avoiding the catastrophe of war, possibilities resulting from the increase in population, the belief in the necessity of the quantitative rise in the standard of living, and from the great impoverishment of the land. 'It is the thoughtless, extravagant, destructive attitude of modern man with regard to his natural environment, from which he has himself grown and on which his existence depends, his remorseless, greedy plundering of the treasures of this environment, his eagerness to defile it for ever with his industrial and human waste products, of which the by-products of atomic installations are only one among many, to defile them to such an extent that perhaps not even our own children, let alone future generations, will be able to live there.' Kennan said on the same occasion that this arises from an 'egocentric attitude, which regards nature as a means to an end and the well-being of present-day man as an independent aim in itself, as though there were neither past nor future, and as though man himself were not a part of nature'. In contrast to that we should recognize 'that it is our duty to hand on to future generations a world just as rich, just as capable of supporting the miracle of life, as we received it'.

Nuclear armament is not the only threat under which we live: its elimination is a necessary but not a sufficient measure. But Kennan's words show too how closely all this is bound together. The murderous attack on God's creation represented by nuclear armament arises from the same 'arrogant and sterile attitude' to nature as the other ways of destruction. The Christian doctrine of creation acquires in our day a new and unprecedented immediacy for the relation of man to the earth. Christians can only make their contribution to the comprehensive re-thinking together with its necessary political and social consequences, if they recognize the indivisibility of their faith in God the Creator and the indivisibility of their resulting responsibility for the earth as the home of future generations. Hence their attitude on the question of nuclear arms acquires the importance of a decisive test.

Such a widening horizon for the tasks of our generation might tempt anew to resignation: it all seems so far beyond the possibilities of governments and governed, of the powerful and the masses. Contemporary writers express this profound discouragement and its reasons more clearly than we usually care to admit in our own minds. 'After the second World War', said Theodor W. Adorno in an interpretation of S. Beckett's *Endspiel* ('End Game') 'everything, including the renascent culture, is destroyed without it being recognized. Mankind lives on in a way in which in fact even the survivors themselves cannot survive, vegetating, crawling about on a heap of ruins, where even the consciousness of their own desolation is of no avail.' This is not the refutation of the Gospel, but the assertion of its unparalleled topicality.

It is just in this world that we are called to confident action to the praise of God. It is just in this world that it becomes clear why this message is not less necessary and not less given—this message with such incomparable content, this message which we, who have survived thus far today to call ourselves Christians, are permitted to serve.

II

WHAT HAS THE CHRISTIAN TO DO WITH POLITICS?

A lecture delivered at the German Evangelical Kirchentag at Stuttgart in 1952

IF WE as Christians are concerned with politics, then so is the Christian Church—there is no doubt about that. Who asks whether we would have it so? The world does not any way. The newspapers, the state authorities, the parties, the political groups, all involve the Church in political life. Whether they ask its advice, or try to use it for their own purposes, or persecute it as hostile to the state, they attribute to the Church a share of political responsibility. And the Lord of the Church himself does not absolve us from responsibility either. In regard to everything that happens in the political sphere he asks us: 'What do you think of that? What have you done about it, good or bad, helpful or harmful?'

Is there then anything at all that can happen in the political sphere that is not of vital import to the Church? Take one example in your own experience in 1945: Refugees arrive in a village. Whom do they meet there? There are country people, natives of the district, residents, the Church is there too, and the parsonage, the parson, the parish records and the church services. The village as an organized community is no longer there; it has not survived, but what about the Christian congregation? Is there really a Christian community there? That is often a matter of life or death for people in distress. With this question in mind it is well to take a look at how men have behaved to one another in the course of history and even in our own day. Wars have been waged on slim pretexts, women and children have been exploited and worked to death, Jews have been boycotted and eventually gassed, the Poles exiled and then the Germans exiled too: threats, hatred and vengeance everywhere. But where is the Christian community in all this? The vital question is not whether they could have prevented it, but whether they took part in it or behaved quite differently. Did they just do what the rest of the world was doing, or did they take quite a different line? That is the urgent question for us today: are we once again going along with the majority, or does the presence of the Christian Church bring a different note into the general hue and cry between East and West, into the mutual recrimination and condemnation, into the daily 'declaration of cold war' and into the economic and party conflicts?

What should be the character of this different conduct of the Christian community? Many of us wish that this question could be answered by directives from leading church authorities, and are inclined to envy the Roman Catholic Church, where there seems to be so much more unity. But in my opinion it is not to some ecclesiastical tribunal that we should appeal, but to the Word of God itself. Or must we suppose that God has left us with no guidance, no light, in this political jungle? In this political fog have we been left dependent on our own tiny light, that is our instinct, on our little bit of natural intelligence, or on our slight political expertise, or even on the dubious lights that other people, the parties, the representatives of various interests, kindle for us? Does the Word of God speak only of salvation and the future life, and has it nothing to say about the affairs of this world?

It does have something very definite to say. It gives us clear and practical guidance even for political life. When we listen to what it says, many questions of detail do indeed remain unanswered, for God has no intention of answering all our questions: his word is not an automatic machine into which you insert a penny and immediately receive a recipe. God wants to leave our intelligence something to do, because that is one of his good gifts, with which he has equipped us for our earthly life. So there are many particular questions left open, and consequently there will be many differences of opinion amongst us. But all these many differences, which have hitherto so deeply disturbed and divided us, are clearly only questions of detail, which God has left to our own intelligence, and which cannot divide us at the deepest level, if we only listen to God's Word together. It speaks quite distinctly about those things concerning which there must not be any difference of opinion among us, about what we have to stand for together, what this 'different behaviour' of the Christian community is in the political field, where the Christian community must not equate itself with the world, as Paul says (Romans 12), nor do what everyone else does, but believe in and witness to the rule of God, even in the political sphere. Inquiring of the Word of God means inquiring of Jesus Christ, and if we ask Jesus Christ, he does not answer with blueprints and schedules, but with his whole life, with the revelation of God's new world in his life and death and resurrection. It is an inexhaustible answer, always the same and yet always quite new to every man, so that every man on every occasion has to hear it afresh for himself.

Let me suggest some things, as I hear the Word today.

1. In Jesus Christ God reveals himself as a God of Peace, as a God who wants to be united with men in peace, and wants to create peace for men, and so he calls us to be men of peace. Where there is a real Christian community there is a force for peace. The world today is filled with the foul poison-fumes of hate. This is increased in the East by the hypocrisy of condemning others as war-mongers and insisting that they themselves are peace-lovers, by the lie about bacteriological warfare in Korea, and by preaching intolerance towards other people's opinions. It is increased here in the West by the general interest in an economic boom, even though it is supported by the building up of arms and by the folly of those who would prefer the policy of the mailed fist to that of patient negotiation, and by the blindness of those who hope to regain their lost territory by war, and in this they are as foolish as the man who sets fire

to his house in order to get into a room that someone has taken from him. We are all susceptible to this poison. One has an account to settle with the Russians; another hates them because they want to take away his factory or his farm; and a third simply hopes that as a result of all this friction with the soviets an end will be made of them once and for all. In all this they cherish the illusion that war could solve the problems that beset the world today, whereas instead it would leave behind an even more unhappy world, and presumably destroy finally all that we hoped to save or conquer. It is impossible for the Christian Church to be neutral about this; it must instead take up a very definite political attitude; it must keep clear of the poisonous miasma of hate; it must avoid the short-sighted folly that toys with war as a political instrument; it must resist to the uttermost any temptation to such ways of thinking; it must call governments and people to peace and oppose openly and courageously any warlike tendencies in the people; it must refuse to support parties in which the idea of war is entertained; it must urge upon its own members in the parties, parliaments and governments that they should look upon their political work as a service to the peace of the world and examine every political decision as to whether it is likely to promote war or peace. It has been said that God has twice struck the weapons of war out of the hands of us Germans, and that therefore we must not take them up again a third time. This statement ignores the possibility that some day perhaps the necessity might again arise even for our German state to form military alliances for its own security. But the statement is right in that God has surely struck the weapons out of our hands twice in order that we should not take them up again lightly and in the same old spirit, with its short-sighted reliance on force and military strength, with its glorification of national egoism and its indifference to right and wrong in our national life. If we have not learned our lesson, then it may well be that God will strike the weapons from our hands a third time and still more terribly, and we ourselves in our obduracy will be the reason for it. Differences of opinion may arise among us as to whether a particular political measure really serves to maintain peace, whether for example the West German defence agreement brings us nearer to peace or war. None of us will be able to pronounce a final judgment on that, since in both courses of action, a 'Yes' or 'No' to the defence treaty, there are obvious dangers to peace. But there should be no disagreement in the Christian Church about the fact that the answer to this particular question should be based on our sense of responsibility for peace. In this at least we should always be united: we in the Christian Church should always bear each other's burdens. Must we not be concerned that in our still sick nation, with our uniforms and weapons, all the spirits of revenge, megalomania, lust for power, conquest, oppression and inhumanity, lurking beneath the surface, are being given another chance? To oppose these spirits we must all be united in the struggle. We ourselves in the Christian Church are by no means safe from them, as history has often shown. But we shall be a source of healing and a force for peace, if we keep ourselves free from them, if we do not give priority to national interests, if we believe that coexistence with other nations is just as important as any advantage for our own, if we keep in view, in political as in personal life, the same rights for others as we demand for ourselves. Each one of us can contribute much to this: we can combat in table talk and in the training of children the evil generalizations about *the* Americans, *the* Russians *the* Czechs, etc., and also the idolizing of national prestige. How this reappeared in all its folly at the Olympic games! Friedrich Wilhelm Förster once said that the favourite pastime of the nations was riding on a roundabout round their own glory. That is something that we Christians should condemn and have nothing to do with. We should not be blind to our own faults and to the virtues and achievements of other nations; we should not be always bemoaning our own fate, but have our eyes open to the needs and sufferings of other nations. That implies that we should continually recognize the Christian Church in all countries as *one*, and encourage liaison with Christians in other lands, not only at ecumenical conferences, but in every congregation, and should tirelessly remind our politicians of their duty to promote peace.

But we cannot work for international peace if we are not men of peace within our own state. In the relationship of the parties to each other, and between the coalition government and the opposition, and—we confess—in the relationship between the denominations, the same evil spirits are at work, endangering our common life, the same generalizations and bitterness, the same miasma of hate. Christians should be bridge-builders: are we really so everywhere? In your congregation there are social democrat and so-called middle-class members of parliament. Is your congregation the bond that unites them, or is it indifferent to their relation to each other? Clearly we have much to do: we must begin at the bottom, every one of us individually. Which are we supporting—peace or discord, bridge-building or disruption?

2. God is a God of righteousness, who loves justice. Thus Christians are men of justice. That does not mean that they are 'barrack-room lawyers'; it does not mean that they are absorbed in legal formalities, but it means that they are men who are concerned about God's law and justice for men. Justice is not merely what is advantageous to the nation, nor is it just what the nation happens to want: it is only learned by listening to the Word of God. God's Word does not give us a universally valid definition of justice, but it gives us guidance which can help us in a particular instance to determine what is just and to distinguish between right and wrong.

(*a*) God as the Creator and Lord has the first and last claim on every man. All human law-making must respect this claim. It does this by asking in respect to every law and ordinance whether it contravenes God's law or not. It does so by not presuming to be the final arbiter of good and evil. It does so by respecting the voice of conscience in men and not compelling them to act against it. A state is only a just state as long as it recognizes this claim of God on men.

(*b*) The Lord God created men first and only after that the state. Therefore he did not create men for the state, but the state for men. In making laws the state has to deal with men already associated together, with mutual obligations which it did not create, but which it should help to maintain, and which therefore are not to be disposed of as it sees fit, and which it cannot just disregard, but has to respect. Marriage, the family, the relation of parents and children, the loyalty of friendship, responsibility for one's neighbour, the destiny of men for eternal life—these are relationships existing before the state. Thus neither the Church nor we individual Christians can stand indifferently aside on questions of educational policy, marriage laws, economic policy, and simply leave it all to the state. The state is neither the supreme nor the sole arbiter of human life. A state is a just state only as long as the power of the state respects these limitations.

(*c*) The Cross of Christ proclaims to us that we men are all in need of forgiveness and are dependent on grace. Even the powerful, the rulers and leaders of the nations, are miserable sinners and fallible men. When the rulers set up their own will in the place of the will of God; when they claim unconditional control over men; when they claim infallibility and persecute every critic of their actions; when they do not acknowledge the laws like other citizens, but set their arbitrary discretion above the law; when the powerful treat with contempt a fundamental law laid down in the constitution; when there is no clear boundary between what is legally permitted and what is legally prohibited, and instead the arbitrary will of the powerful punishes what is permitted and condones illegalities, there man is setting the lie of his infallibility against the Cross of Christ. A just state only exists where the power of the state restricts and controls the powerful, and where the rulers acknowledge God's eternal law.

We Christians have a responsibility to see that the power of the state recognizes its limitations and obligations. Living in a country that claims to be a constitutional state, i.e. that recognizes these limitations and obligations, we share responsibility for seeing that it remains a constitutional state. That means that we share responsibility for seeing that it does not fall a victim to any tyrannical power attacking it from outside and trying to set up the arbitrary rule of force in place of law. We thus share responsibility for the defence of the constitutional state, and as part of this responsibility it may well happen that armed force, even the recourse to war, becomes part of obedience to the will of God. In my opinion therefore the will of God does not permit us to be pacifists on principle. The same Christian who is a man of peace will affirm the responsibility of his government for the defence of the constitutional state, and will support it in doing so. Thus he will train himself in the use of arms, and in case of need, i.e. when it is really a question of the defence of the constitutional state, he will let himself be called up.

But the constitutional state is never threatened only from outside: it is always threatened from the inside also. To look only at the threat from outside—at present from the East—is easily to become blind to the dangers from within. We ourselves are the danger from within, for in us all there is the inclination to fight injustice with injustice. We in Germany have to learn over again to hear the voice of justice, even when it is inconvenient. We must recognize the obligation to truth in political life also, even towards a political opponent. We must recognize the duty to stand courageously for right even when the powerful violate it. Whenever power does not serve justice, but sets justice aside, resistance is a Christian duty. The events of the 20th of July 1944 should always be a reminder of that. When Hitler declared: 'Bolshevism is terror and can only be fought with terror', many people in Germany and probably many of us here realized the truth. Actually that statement was the real surrender to bolshevism. It meant complete identification with the thing we were supposed to be fighting against, until at last only the colours and phrases were different, but not the systems themselves. Today there are temptations urging us in the same direction. Once again many people are prepared to treat anyone who steps out of line politically with every means of defamation, lies and violence, and to deprive him of his rights, and many would like to apply Hitler's methods to the communists.

That is the way to transform a just state into an unjust state. We Christians ought to be a barrier holding back the state from this slippery slope. We must recognize and proclaim clearly that terror is in fact no protection against terror. Only justice is, even if it is uncomfortable and seems less effective. To defend justice and freedom by unjust means does more harm to our state than all the communists could do. It conjures up evil spirits, which it is impossible to exorcize, and which destroy the very thing that it would defend.

3. God in Christ is a God of mercy. Christians are therefore men of mercy and this in a twofold sense: they are men who know that they themselves are in need of forgiveness, and men who are ready to forgive. Has forgiveness anything to do with politics? A very great deal! We can see that in our own situation. The question of forgiveness is inseparable from the much discussed question of guilt, that still produces in many of us a violent reaction. Today we are striving for sovereignty; we are glad that the other nations need us again, and we feel that the past should be written off, since the others are no angels either, and had enough blots on their own copybooks. It would be a misfortune, however, if in this way we sidetracked the question of guilt. Why? Because for one thing nothing has been achieved, if we forget what the Germans have done, as long as the others do not forget it. In that way it goes on smouldering and poisons our relations with the other nations. The others cannot forget it as long as we are content just to cover it up and behave as though there were nothing particular between them and us. The evil that was done by our side and in the name of the German people must not be excused or minimized, but must be a reason for us to ask the other nations—particularly Israel—for forgiveness. Only so shall we recover our national honour. Only so shall we cease to be an object of hatred, contempt and suspicion. Every visit abroad, every conversation with other nationals who have been our victims, confirms this.

But this is important not only because of our relations with the other nations, but also for our own sake. Our attitude to the question of guilt shows whether we have heard the voice of

God speaking through what we have been through. He has humbled us. Have we learned humility? Have at least we Christians in Germany learned humility as Germans? Have we accepted in our hearts what our brethren confessed in the name of the Protestant Church in Germany before the representatives of the universal Church in the so-called Stuttgart Confession in 1945? 'Before I was afflicted I went astray: but now I have kept thy word' (Ps. 119.67). Only by letting oneself be humbled does one learn from experience: he alone draws the right conclusion from disaster. He is not so much concerned about the misdeeds of others as about what evil he himself has done, what he has himself contributed to his own calamity, so that he can learn from it a lesson for the future. We Germans are always in danger of becoming arrogant in prosperity and of cringing in misfortune. Only by accepting the will of God and letting ourselves be humbled by his word can we avoid both these things. Our attitude to the question of guilt determines whether or not we can face the future as a nation that has learned its lesson. And here the attitude of the Christian Church in Germany is of immediate and crucial importance. We cannot help it if many Germans remain impenitent and obdurate, but we Christians can, as a 'creative minority' (Lilje), exert a powerful influence to assure that our nation will not again be regarded with horror by others. We do not want to be a terror to other nations, and that includes the eastern nations. We cannot find our way into the future, if we do not recognize how large a part of the blame we Germans bear for the tragic condition of the modern world. Without God men do their utmost to forget the evil they themselves have done and to remember only the guilt of others. Christians must adopt the diametrically opposite attitude: we must try to forget the crimes of the others and keep in mind the frightful things that have been done in the name of and by members of our nation. Instead of forgetting them we would seek forgiveness for them. Only so can we hope that such things will not happen again. Only then shall we be ready to bear and surmount with patience and fortitude the heavy burdens that are laid upon our nation today, without dreaming of vengeance, and the military conquest of the eastern territories, and new power politics, thereby making the disaster still worse.

We have only instanced a few important points: many others have not been mentioned. But the direction in which the Word of God points us has no doubt been made clear. If we can be united on these fundamental questions, if the realization of these truths leads us to see our common duty, then we can render an irreplaceable service to our nation in these days. Who is better able than we to understand this clearly? Who will do it, if we do not? In respect to individual questions of detail and questions of personal judgment, there will be differences of opinion among us. It has never been promised that we shall always find a common answer to every practical question. Particular measures can often be judged very differently, as the violent discussion about the West German defence contribution shows. But is not the important thing the spirit in which a plan is decided on and carried through? On that depends very often what consequences it brings. It is therefore important to distinguish between questions of personal judgment as to which measures are advisable and which are not, and fundamental questions of principle. The answer we give to every question of personal judgment is influenced by our fundamental attitude, and so the Christian faith affects even these decisions. The will of God always has to be worked out in specific decisions, where we have to rely on our own intelligence to decide what actions best fulfil the will of God as we have discerned it. Just as long as we are united in willingness and eagerness to listen for God's will for his Church, it will be found that we are like-minded even where we advocate different courses of action. Then the Christian faith will bear a common and effective witness even in political affairs. In contrast to the so-called 'law unto itself' existing in political affairs, and in contrast to the view that in politics the only right course is the result of the only right point of view and the ruthless furtherance of one's own interests, and that the only proper method is the ruthless use of all available means, we Christians will hear and advocate together: the blessing of God is more important than results, for it is on that blessing that we live. Only what is blessed is durable even in politics. Short-sighted fools keep their eyes on results, but those who are wise through the Word of God think of the blessing. Blessing comes only through seeking and listening to the will of God, even in politics. So God's Word is 'not a vain thing for us, because it is our life' (Deut. 32.47). If we choose the path of repentance and turning over a new leaf, even in politics, then we choose life. If we persistently choose the right and not evil and terror, then we choose life. If as far as in us lies we choose peace everywhere, we choose life.

III

THE CHRISTIAN BETWEEN EAST AND WEST

A lecture delivered at the Congress of the Christian Peace Service at Nürnberg-Stein in August 1950 and at the Evangelical Academy at Tutzing.

WE SHALL confine ourselves strictly to our theme, which is concerned with Christians, i.e. with each one of us individually. We are therefore not so much concerned with the *Church* in its attitude to the disturbing problem of today, the problem of East and West, for like each one of us, the Church is exposed to the persuasion of both sides. Both sides want the Church as an ally, and thus recognize, surprisingly perhaps, that it is still an institution with a considerable influence over the masses. The West tries to convince the Church that resistance to the East is in its own interest, and is indeed a question of survival, and that Western civilization is its creation, with which it stands or falls. The appeal of the communist East is no less powerful: its tactics indeed by no means suggest that it desires the liquidation of the Church. It too tries to win the Church over: it commends itself to it as the party of progress, as the way to an equitable social order. It reminds the Church of its mission to stand up for the oppressed. It draws attention to the failure of the Church in this task hitherto, and appeals to it to turn over a new leaf at last. It attempts to split the 'reactionary' elements within the Church from the 'progressive' and to make peace with the people who claim allegiance to the Church. We must be clear about one thing: both sides want what is *ours*, but not *us*. They have their own interests in mind when they appeal to the Church.

A heated debate is going on among us about this appeal, as to which path the Church should choose. The decision of the Vatican on one side and of the Patriarch of Moscow on the other, indicates the conflicting possibilities. Even within the Protestant section of Christianity there are wide dfferences of opinion and several tentative alignments, ranging from the disunited 'religious socialists' to the widely misunderstood attitude of Martin Niemöller and Karl Barth, or at the other extreme the decisive attitude of Emil Brunner. It is certainly necessary for all of us to consider what the attitude of the Church as a whole should be, what attitude we should advise its leaders and official representatives to take, and from what attitude we should dissuade them. But that must not supplant or displace the other consideration, namely how this question affects each one of us, and what each of us can do about it.

The question is put to us in the form of a blunt alternative, a harsh either/or, summed up in the geographical label East/West. This must not tempt us to think of it as a geographically conditioned alternative, such as often happens in historical and philosophical speculations, which then tend to assume a permanent conflict between East and West. It is much more a question of two fronts, recognizable at the moment geographically, and extending along a frontier between two powers, that is still disputed only in a few places, and at the same time there are two political and philosophical fronts which cut right through all nations. In so far as it is a conflict between two powers, Stalin's formula about the possibility of co-existence of the two systems gave some hope, which to many people today seems out of date. It presupposes mutual trust and non-interference, for which there is no readiness today on either side. Moreover the experience of history gives cause for scepticism about the possibility of a dualism of peace instead of just an armed truce. Is not a cold war bound sooner or later to turn into a hot war as the result of the inevitable deterioration into a struggle for power? The threat is all the greater since the imperialist conflict is at the same time also an ideological one, in which each half of the world regards its own side as religious crusaders. Hence the difficult question, which appeared as long ago as 1939, is today even more difficult to answer, namely whether in actual fact we were faced with a struggle for power, in which ideology was cynically introduced as an instrument of propaganda, or whether on the contrary it was really a religious conflict, in which power served to support the ideas—a question which probably can never be completely answered.

The Christian finds himself faced with the conflict of these two giants, still at present a cold war (and it is to be hoped not developing tomorrow into a hot war), being appealed to by both powers to side with them, and he wonders what attitude he should take towards them. But what sort of person is a Christian?

Following the New Testament we can venture on a simple definition: a Christian is a slave who has been transferred to a new Master. He has been redeemed, so that he is free from his old master, to whom like all other men he was subject, and has been purchased by a new good Master, to whom he now belongs entirely, so that on the one hand none of the former masters, and thus no earthly power, neither men nor death nor his own sin, can touch or harm him any longer, and on the other hand his duties are now given him solely by this new Master, together with the equipment for them. These two things, his being redeemed and purchased, must now be clearly evident in his attitude to the conflict between the great world powers.

Two kinds of freedom result from being a Christian.

1. Because we belong absolutely to our new Master, Christ, we are no longer identified for weal or woe with one of the two world powers. We are free from the pressure of self-interest. A factory owner or a big farmer may be predisposed by his interests in favour of one camp, while a working man may regard the other camp as representing his interests, but a Christian, whether he lives on dividends or on a daily wage, is free from the obligation in which his material interests might determine his decisions.

2. Directly connected with this: a Christian is free from

the domination of fear. As long as we are afraid, our flesh tries to defend itself, and in its fear uses even the Gospel as a weapon of self-defence, for fear justifies every means. But the redeemed slave must know that his former masters cannot do anything to him: they can neither help nor destroy him. As long as the slave was bound by interest and motivated by fear, he saw the conflict between the two world powers from the point of view of a partisan of one side or the other, and so he tended to regard the conflict as absolute, a conflict of justice against injustice, of good against evil, of light against darkness.

Now he can no longer do this. Now there is for him only one ultimate conflict and that is not localized in Washington and Moscow, any more than in Wittenberg and Rome: it is within himself. It is the conflict between the sinner and God, a conflict that has been resolved by the miracle of the atonement. What then of all these other conflicts?

There are two alternatives: the first, particularly when the conflicts are seen as absolute, is that they are conflicts between unredeemed men, who are giving vent to their hatred in religious, ideological or nationalistic forms. As such they represent no more than the various forms of behaviour characteristic of unregenerate men, arrogant crusades of self-idolatry and self-salvation. They have a great deal more in common than they imagine, and one thing is true of them all without distinction —that they have come short of the glory of God (Rom. 3.23). It is a game in which the Christian can no longer take part, and which is fundamentally alien and without interest to him.

The second alternative is that they are conflicts that have not been abolished by the atonement and which Christ has allowed to persist, just as after the resurrection he allowed the earth to remain as it was, and which extend even into the Church. The fact that in the Church there was no longer to be any conflict between Greek and barbarian, master and slave, Jewish Christian and gentile Christian (Col. 3.11) and yet these conflicts persisted, meant that the differences were blunted: they no longer created a final separation, nor were they an obstacle to brotherhood, but rather provided a stimulus to it. We speak deliberately of conflicts and not just surviving distinctions, for we do not want to minimize their actual starkness. They are a part of the truly heavy burden of the world that the Christian still has to bear, and their effect is always of conflict, just as surely as that between Onesimus and Philemon. There was not only a distinction in this case, but a real conflict of interests, which after all drove Onesimus to flight and made it necessary for Paul to intercede for him. The Christian is not outside these conflicts: he is in them and may even be committed to one of the sides. The important thing however is his attitude within them.

1. He sees the conflict blunted. He may well belong to one of the contending parties, he supports their cause and their interests, he agrees with their case and tries to get it recognized. But he does not accept the demands of his party wholesale and unconditionally. He does not belong to it body and soul. He has brethren on the other side also, and that makes him keep looking afresh at the other side and considering their case too. He does not think in terms of the 'friend-foe' category, which Carl Schmitt worked out as the basic category of political conflict. The disastrous thing about Carl Schmitt's idea, by which he justified in theory the actions of the National Socialist state, was that his analysis of its political behaviour, which was certainly determined by 'friend-foe' relationship, became for him subconsciously the norm of political action, and so the objectivity of political behaviour was dependent on the unrestricted and absolute validity of the 'friend-foe' category. Thus he legitimized in fascist terms what Leninism had been doing for a long time, glorifying 'intransigeance' and violently opposing every form of 'conciliation'. The conflict of parties and programmes thus produced the most important and complete division of mankind—a division which to the Christian, however, was only secondary. To him the conflict never destroyed the sense of community; to him the human being on the other side was not submerged in the enemy; to him the conflict did not abrogate all other ties and duties towards those on the other side; to him these endure. He can and must even disregard time and

again the fact that his opponent is his opponent, and in the way in which he pursues the conflict he is not subject to the dictates of self-interest, which would justify every means. He has to obey the orders of his new Master, and these may often be contrary to his own interest. The 'friend-foe' category belongs to the primeval forest. In the West Christianity has built a barrier against its validity, and all the traditional rules of chivalry in war; institutions like the Red Cross, the Hague Convention, derive from this. In communism and fascism men are very busy removing this barrier. The immediate duty of a Christian is to help to rebuild it against the encroaching jungle.

2. The Christian sees the conflict with disillusioned eyes. He knows that it is not a question of selfless fighting for the triumph of the good, but simply and frankly for power and prestige. He sees the material interests concealed behind the ideas expressed in eloquent public statements. He is irritated by the moral fog: he wants a clear admission from his own party that in this conflict it is every one for himself, so that it is not a conflict of love. (For this reason Christians should avoid talking about the 'defence of the Christian West'. To non-Christians western Christianity may well be part of our higher culture, which they wish to defend by force. Christians must know that what is Christian cannot be defended as a possession, but is always witnessed to only in selfless sacrifice. Hence western Christianity cannot be defended at all, but only lived.)

3. The Christian is unprejudiced in this conflict. We call a judge prejudiced, who assumes from the outset that one of the parties is right. The Christian however is free to see and to say what truth and right is on the other side, and likewise the wrong on his own side. He is not frightened by propagandist considerations. He is not obliged to vilify the other side and to glorify his own. He is able to recognize whatever good things are going on on the other side. He can be glad if it turns out that even those on the other side are not as bad as they are made out to be. He will not conceal the wrong on his own side from considerations of solidarity; the dirt in his own nest worries him just as much as that in the nest of others. He can always look

at the matter in dispute from the other side also; he can thus act really objectively in the political conflict and, what Carl Schmitt and his pragmatical followers in all camps always forget, he can exercise justice by finding out what is right and just on both sides.

This has two consequences in political action.

1. Because the Christian does not swear blind allegiance to his party, because his party is not his religion, because he adheres to his party conditionally and does not regard it as always and in every way right, because he therefore can never be a fanatic, he will always be regarded by his own side as 'unreliable', he will give offence to them and be uncomfortable. H. J. Iwand's statement: 'The Confessing Church is always in opposition' contains an essential law for the political action of the Christian.

2. The Christian is a man of reconciliation even in political life. That does not mean that he indolently favours peace at any price or yields on principle. He will always bear in mind the important difference between forgiving and giving way. He is by no means incapable of clear demarcation and stout resistance. He can be ordered to fight stubbornly, to wage war and not yield one step. If the report is true that in concluding the Munich agreement in 1938 Chamberlain and Halifax were actuated by strong religious motives, it is questionable whether it was a right Christian insight that impelled them to maintain peace at any price. But it is quite definite, as Augustine so aptly said, that for the Christian even the hardest fight has peace for its objective, not the destruction of the enemy, nor even his unconditional surrender, but to persuade him to a just settlement. We often discuss far too casuistically the question of morality in politics (whether a statesman should lie or break agreements, and so on). In reality that is all decided by the fundamental question of what the conflict means to him. Is it a way to peace with his opponent or to the destruction of his life or at least of his will to resist? And what does his opponent mean to him? Is he nothing more than an enemy, to be destroyed by any and every means, or is he someone with whom he has to and wants

to live, and with respect to whom he may use only such methods as will not make living together tomorrow impossible, someone who is fighting, as are those on either side, with only relative right or wrong? That is true everywhere, where the Christian is involved in politics, and we all are, whether we occupy positions of leadership or are like grains of corn among the mass of the population, with which the politician always has to reckon.

How real these apparently very general factors actually are, which we have so far described, is evident as soon as we consider the kind of conflict with the official demands that a Christian has to face in the eastern states, if he adopts the Christian attitude to the East-West problem already described. But there is sufficient evidence that a Christian can find himself in a no less dangerous situation in the West today or tomorrow, if he behaves as a Christian in political life. At the same time such action might well have immediate and perhaps momentous political significance. The psychology of the cold war can only be understood by recognizing the effect of the demon of fear upon the leaders and followers alike in both East and West. A Christianity that is truly Christian creates barriers against a preventive war, removes the inevitability of the development from a cold war to a hot one, destroys the hypocrisy of the crusader motive, demands the utilization of every opportunity to remove danger points, checks the questionable force of prestige, which always misses chances of agreement because of an alleged 'point of no return'. But if God in his righteous judgment allows the transition from cold to hot war to happen, it will be of crucial importance to the countless victims of this war, whether they meet in the opposite camp men who have this Christian outlook.

So far we have considered the Christian as standing *between* East and West, i.e. his attitude towards both camps is that of a stranger and a pilgrim (1 Peter 2.11). He is not at home in either camp, and yet is involved in the conflict between them. Our position is not *between* East and West in indifferent neutrality: our citizenship in heaven (Phil. 3.20) does not mean that we can look on like inhabitants of another planet. We all already live in the East or in the West. This association, depending on where we live, is a limitation which it is most important to consider. Because it is often taken insufficiently into consideration, Christians in the two halves of the world misunderstand and mistrust each other and fail to understand their opposite decisions or to recognize them as being Christian at all. We all have idealism in our blood. We continually confuse Christian obedience with the implementation of an idea—in our case the idea of a Christian state—and so we regard as a denial and breach of our community the decisions of other people, who do not see their duty as the realization of our common idea, although it might well be that they see these decisions as their own way of obedience. The Christian in the East finds that our common Lord makes different demands upon him. His political responsibility, from which he is not absolved, takes a different form from that of Christians in the West. Whether a totalitarian régime is just a subject for discussion or is an actual system under which we live makes a profound difference to the form of Christian obedience required of us, and how we carry it out. We shall not cease to ask serious questions concerning each other, but we shall only venture to judge each other very cautiously and reluctantly. If we forget that, we must not be surprised if our brother in the other camp does not recognize the voice of our common Lord in our reproaches, demands and imputations, but only the voice of our party. For this reason I shall describe separately the position of the Christian in the East and in the West, and assess the political responsibility of the Christian in the West so that no immediate conclusions can be drawn as to what the Christian in the East should do.

What does it mean to live as a Christian in the East? A few points may make this clear.

1. The Christian in the East is atoning for the sin of the Church. Its shortcomings are continually being pointed out to him. Everything that it has ever neglected, every wrong it has ever condoned is listed. Some of these Christians have revolted, declaring that they cannot condone the injustice in the world, as the Church has always been able to do. The Christian cannot

deny that in many of them there is a feeling of revolt against the social injustices, which should have been the lively concern of the Church. He simply cannot defend the Church. He sees himself called to a revolution in which the old guilt-laden Church must give way to a new regenerate one. Hence as a Christian he cannot simply long to leave the East to go to the West, for he feels the greatest distrust of the 'Christian' West also. We in the West must be very careful not to assume that he wants to do so. We shall rather have to consider that every alliance with western injustice that we enter into here increases the burden of the sin of the Church which he has to bear over there.

2. The Christian in the East has been deprived of his freedom as something anti-social. The only freedom still left to him is the freedom of judgment. He is completely thrown back on Christ. He is sustained by trust in his word. His freedom consists in his refusal to let anybody stop him being the slave of his new Master. The personal freedom that the West boasts of against the East, is the freedom of association, the freedom of the customer in the store, who has the privilege of choice. We can choose any day without hindrance amongst the wide selection of philosophies and ways of life, and we are so glad of this freedom of choice that many people think they have to defend the essential dignity of man by just this freedom of choice. It was significant that recently at the great Intellectual Congress in Berlin, where the word 'freedom' was heard a dozen times an hour, scarcely anybody except the Catholic Eugen Kogon and the Protestant Denis de Rougemont reminded them that the essence of personal freedom was responsibility. The freedom of choice, which the West actually has to defend today, can be simply paraphrased as independence from the tyranny of another person. I am not absolutely free, but rather, while subject to the law of the state and to all sorts of influences and liabilities, I am nevertheless free from the arbitary interference in my life on the part of a more powerful person. In the East a man is deprived of this freedom. He is thrown back more completely on the freedom which Christ gives to his redeemed slave, and

which no one can take away from him. Thus he is free, not in the precarious protection of dissociation, but only in his union with Christ. This is his existential advantage over the western Christian.

3. The Christian in the East is the only one to whom the Church of Christ is really his living space. He can no longer live outside the Church and without it. In the Church alone he finds an area in which man is not passed over, where his dignity is respected, where men trust one another, where he can venture to speak openly and the secrecy of the confessional is vitally important, and where he can still find understanding and above all forgiveness. In a very real sense he lives on forgiveness, since he can no longer live on the illusion of his respectability, for he too, the Christian, is untruthful. Every day he is driven to lies, evasions and deceptions, and he can only be a man, when he finds forgiveness.

4. The Christian in the East learns the wonderful purifying power of truth. In a world in which lying is ordered by the government and affects him also again and again, he is invited again and again to dare to tell the truth. He sees signs and wonders when he ventures to tell the truth and he experiences the profound comfort of Christ, when he suffers for it.

5. The Christian in the East 'seeks the peace of the city'. The exhortation which the prophet Jeremiah wrote to the exiled Jews in Babylon, is true for him also. He does his civic duty, he takes part in social reconstruction, yet he finds himself continually faced with the disquieting question as to what the 'peace of the city' consists in, whether it does not demand first of all the collapse of the existing system, whether he should not participate in efforts to bring about this collapse, and so whether by fulfilling his obligations he is not doing precisely the wrong thing, namely helping to stabilize the existing anti-Christian system. He finds the duty of resistance and sabotage suggested to him. He knows too, that actually the extreme case might arise where the 'peace of the city' can only be found in total resistance to the existing régime in defiance of the law (20th of July 1944). But Christ frees the Christian from the 'domination

of logical consequence'. Placed between Romans 13 and Acts 13 he can remain loyal and obedient to the system of government, which God has permitted, and refuse the alleged duty of resistance, which nevertheless may in the extreme case become his duty tomorrow. Although the Christian in the West cannot wish to see the extension of the totalitarian system, and must therefore try to prevent it, because it rejects the supreme claim of the divine command, yet the Christian in the East can obey the totalitarian state, which God in his providence has permitted, in so far as the express command of God in a concrete case does not order otherwise.

But what does it mean to live as a Christian in the West today? The exhortation to 'seek the peace of the city' applies to us Christians in the West too, but what does that actually mean for us? It is easy to draw a false conclusion—that the practical atheism of the West and the theoretical atheism of the East are both equally godless, and that both systems competing for our support are walking in that darkness in which all cats are grey. The East has social justice and inhibits freedom; the West has freedom and sins against social justice. The comparison is however inaccurate. While the East has abolished freedom, it has in reality lost also the very social justice that it was once so concerned about. It is not socialist in the sense that socialism was once promised. The change in the nature of socialism that occurred in the transition from Marx via Lenin to Stalin cannot be better expressed than in the words of a reporter from the eastern zone: 'The working class here is now the deadly enemy of communism.' A proper sense of contrition in the West does not mean forgetting or minimizing differences which still exist. The fact that here in the West the basis of individual justice still exists, about which Luther once said that it is more important than our daily bread; the fact that personal liberty in the sense already indicated as independence from the tyranny of another person, still exists, and that a man's personal responsibility is not denied on principle, and that it is still possible to strive freely for social improvement—all these are differences which the fourth petition of the Lord's Prayer teaches us to value as God's gifts. We should not boast of these differences, but we should be ungrateful to the patience of God, who has permitted us to possess them still, if we denied them or disregarded them. For that reason we cannot wish the East to dominate the West. If God permitted that, we should have no right to complain; it would be a merited judgment on the abominable way in which his good gifts are misused in the West. We should have to accept this judgment as a penance, but we have no need to bring it about. The threat of it should instead make us determined to ward it off by making better use of God's gifts. The pertinent question however nowadays is whether we may resist this threatened judgment by defending the West. We are reminded of the example of Jeremiah, who condemned the defence of Jerusalem against Nebuchadnezzar as a sinful resistance against the judgment of God. On the other hand which one of us has today the prophetic authority to oppose those who are responsible for the defence of the West on the strength of the protest of Jeremiah? Are we not constantly and rightly engaged in protecting ourselves from all sorts of ills (illness, crime, etc.) which we have to accept as judgments when our defences fail?

By our resistance to the domination of the East over the West we are of course affirming the West, but only in so far as we affirm the gifts which are still ours through the patience of God. We do not accept the West entirely, not as it is. We do not want the West to remain as it is, but no word of our criticism will lead us towards the East or commend the communist (i.e. totalitarian) system as a remedy or as an expedient. Hence we shall not necessarily agree with every means of defence of the West, nor of every ally. No word of our criticism of the East will lead us towards fascism or justify fascism as a means of defence. For example, western politicians will have to take into account in their calculations the presence of Franco, but if they are Christians they will not attempt to justify in retrospect the horrors of Spanish fascism any more than Hitler's anti-communist atrocities. What are we to say when we read in a Christian periodical: 'In the case of Spain, have we not been looking all the time at the mote without trying to see the beam that it has removed from its eye just in time? Where would Europe be today if Spain had become a communist democracy in 1936?' These words, which express a widespread argument, are the scandal of modern Christianity, for which the Christian in the East is having to atone. Georges Bernanos in one of his posthumous essays quite rightly challenges: 'We should imagine how a victorious Mussolini would have been honoured in the Vatican.' We would add, a victorious Hitler in the Protestant churches in Germany!

But here, of course, there is a most important difference between the non-totalitarian West and the totalitarian East. Accepting the East means accepting the system entirely, including the very things which a Christian cannot accept, the distortion of the state, the abrogation of rights and the degradation of human beings. The acceptance of the West is not the acceptance of a system. It is not, as is often said, a misfortune, but a good thing, that the West has no ideology to set against that of the East. It is not the assertion of laissez-faire liberalism, or of capitalism, of social injustice, nationalism, armaments profits, the colonial system, or total or semi fascism in Spain or South Korea, but it is the assertion of the possibilities that still exist for us to fight against these evils. What we denounce in the West are evils that we are not in any case compelled to defend, but which we can condemn openly as evils, and which derive not so much from a system as from the sinful nature of man, and which do not therefore require a complete condemnation of the West any more than a Frenchman would condemn his French culture and way of life just because within it he cannot ignore the Place Pigalle.

These facts must be faced frankly. On the basis of them our politicians are right in regarding as a task committed to them in the ballot box to see to it that the East does not dominate us. They have the right to expect our support and not sabotage. The question, however, that torments us, particularly today, is whether this resistance should include the use of armed force. The threat is a military one, and so it must be resisted militarily.

In principle that cannot be gainsaid, assuming that the Church has been right throughout in its relative, conditional and limited justification of the use of the sword. Anyone who today decided to refuse military service must remember that the creation of armed forces and the threat of war do not put to him simply the question as to what he as an individual will do, and what he feels God calls him to do, but also the other question what he could honestly commend to the responsible statesmen like Attlee and Truman as their duty in the present world situation, and whether he really believes he can honestly demand that they should stop building up arms. Here of course the grotesque element in this world situation becomes clear, that among the leaders of the East the basic motive for aggression and armament seems to be not so much aggressive intentions as fear of encirclement and intervention—a fear certainly rooted deeply in the Soviet view of the world and not just produced by the measures adopted in the West. For us Germans all this focuses in the contentious question of rearmament. The press is daily setting out the reasons for and against. Influential voices (Martin Niemöller, Reinhold Schneider) appeal to us as Christians to renounce finally all reliance on the sword and any resort to arms, and to accept and retain the disarmament of Germany as a sign given to us by God. We must not reject this appeal out of hand on specious political arguments. It must be a warning to us against relying too easily on arms for our safety, as Christianity has so often done. The question in my mind, in view of all this, is whether we should not have to accept also the military defence of the West. The statement of the Berlin Synod in April 1950 on peace is neither out of date nor unpractical. Even the obligation of the Church to intercede for and defend the conscientious objectors is still operative, for it does not depend, as some people think, on whether the whole Church rejects a particular war as 'unjust'. The Church does not regulate the individual conscience, and so it has to protect its individual member, even if it as a whole cannot support his decision. But we have to ask the conscientious objector and everyone who demands the witness of the Church against rearmament, whether they are allowing this freedom of conscience to others, and so whether they understand that different decisions on this question cannot destroy our community in the Church.

Recently it was stated significantly that there were two dangers threatening Europe—communism and anti-communism. The danger of an anti-communist intervention on the part of the Church, such as is often demanded today, is that it represents primarily a negative defensive attitude—just saying 'No' to communism without revealing the defects of the West. The revival of the anti-communist front that Hitler introduced in 1933 is an act of impenitence and paves the way to fascism. We should be more concerned with whatever positive action we can take than with what we have to defend ourselves against negatively. The refugee problem is a clear example. Today we insist that this is a world problem and cannot be solved by us Germans alone, and that is true, but we appeal to the world before we ourselves have done everything that we might do. Neither our governments nor parliaments and parties nor the Church give a strong lead towards solidarity and mutual responsibility, which would unite in one common fate and one common sacrifice those who have been lucky and those who have been unfortunate. Men cling naturally to a superstitious belief in negative measures; the Christian is aware of priorities in what we do. He knows that only the positive can heal. If the zeal that many Christians feel they should manifest for the defence against communism were directed to the positive things that ought to be done in the West, then the defence itself would look more believable from a Christian standpoint. It will be useful, therefore, if we in conclusion make clear in more detail the responsibility which we have as Christians in the West.

1. It is part of the responsibility of the Church and of the individual Christian to treasure the material goods that God has preserved to us and to teach others to do so. As we teach the children to ask for and to give thanks for our daily bread, so we must include in our petition and thanksgiving justice

and liberty in political and social life. Part of the guilt that our evangelical Christianity has to bear in relation to pre-war Germany is that in the then existing crisis of democracy and the constitutional state it did not give a sufficiently strong and instructive lead about the treasuring of these goods—indeed it took an active part in the undermining of democracy and the achievements of liberal ideas of freedom and justice—and that it encouraged the fetish of submission to authority that comes so easily to us Germans, instead of guiding us towards an integrated social life. This undermining process is already going on among us again in spite of the fact that we are enjoying the extraordinary miracle of being able to build up a constitutional state under the protection of law and liberty, instead of going straight from the degradation of the Hitler régime to that of Stalin.

2. This attitude of grateful appreciation means among other things that we have no longer any illusions about the real nature of every form of totalitarianism. The proper non-involvement of the Christian does not mean whitewashing what is going on over there, or representing judgments about it as interested western provocation, or believing that anyway things are not so bad. They *are* so bad. But there is a great difference between explaining for ourselves and others the good reasons for rejecting the eastern system, and the sort of provocation which is willing to use every means to unloose hatred. Politicians and generals are hard to dissuade from the erroneous opinion, disproved by the experience of many wars, that hatred is essential for mobilizing a determined will to resist. There are already appearing in our newspapers horrific accounts of the atrocities committed by the North Koreans, whereas at the beginning of the conflict a few small notices slipped shamefacedly through in a few newspapers, that for example in the two days following the beginning of the North Korean attack no fewer than two thousand people were 'liquidated' by the South Koreans on suspicion of espionage. The war was fought with frightful crimes on both sides, and we must be more concerned with checking injustice on our own side than with

justifying it by real or supposed atrocities on the other side. To make it clear for us today by an example from the past: The Christian in the West loses what is entrusted to him, if he allows himself to be persuaded to paint Hitler white in order to paint Stalin black.

3. In the development of future events it will therefore depend to a large extent on the attitude of Christian men whether the West escapes the danger that in the conflict with eastern totalitarianism it becomes itself totalitarian, and thus in the defence of freedom loses freedom itself. As long as we refuse to think in the friend/foe category, as long as we do not let ourselves be governed by total hatred and its logical consequences, as long as we do not allow the few remaining strands connecting us with people and institutions in the eastern half of the world to be severed in the name of political consistency, as long as we do not exchange the non-involvement of the Christian for the blinkers of party membership, just so long are we rendering to the western world the service that it needs in order not to come under the law of its opponents, and at the end of the struggle to have lost the very thing that the conflict was about.

4. Karl Barth recently ended a conversation about a suggested anti-communist intervention by the Church with this wise statement: 'Anti-communism is the product of fear, and the most important message that the Church can proclaim today is, "Fear not".' The Christian has been given eternal life by his new Master, and so any imaginable fear of the future has no longer any ultimate terror for him. Anxiety lives on the ultimate terror. What is this ultimate terror? The ultimate terror threatens the loss of what makes life worth living; it threatens that we shall not be able to endure the future, and that our only fate is despair, and suicide our last escape. The Lord looks after his redeemed slave. No one can tear him from his hand. Nothing that happens can be for us the ultimate terror. But the Christian understands the fear in the heart of his fellow men. He understands it firstly because he has experienced it. Which of us does not feel it creep over him when, in view

of his past experience, he thinks of all the things the future may hold—hunger, nightly air raids, arrests, hours of hell in the trenches, frozen children, raped women. We are only free from fear as long as we are continually being freed from it, and it cannot produce in us the ultimate terror as long as we keep our eyes, not on what may come, but on him who is to come, and who is present with us now, Jesus Christ. The Christian understands fear secondly because he knows that apart from Christ, apart from the Gospel, there is only the ultimate terror left. He knows that today apart from Christ a man can only conceal fear with frivolity and self-narcosis or with a forced optimism as the Marxist tries to do, but he cannot escape it. The Christian sees him reading above the gateway of the future the gloomy words of Mahomet, that Wilhelm Raabe put at the beginning of his 'Abu Telfan': 'If you knew what I know, you would weep much and laugh little.' He, on the other hand, witnesses to the new life in Christ. He testifies in his speech and conduct, and also in the calmness, conciliation and firmness of his political actions, to the way in which the resurrection of Christ has reversed this saying: 'If you knew what I know, you would laugh more and not weep so much, even in the year 1950 in the situation between East and West.'

IV

THE CHURCH AND MARXISM IN THE EUROPEAN CRISIS

Points from an address to a session of the Franco-German Council of Brethren at Bievres in June 1951

1. WHY DOES the Church of Jesus Christ share the blame for the present situation in Europe?

Not because the fate of Christendom depends on the fate of Europe.

Not because the western form of 'Christian culture' is the only possible and permanently valid one.

Not because this western form of Christian culture is not open to criticism by the Gospel.

Not therefore because it is desirable to restore the relation between Church and State that existed in the Middle Ages.

But (*a*) because the Church is present in this Europe, and cannot be there without being held responsible to God for its way of life and its contribution to the life of the people who live there.

(*b*) because of the special historical connection of Christianity with this Europe, with its faults and its achievements, and also because of its special influence on humanity as a whole.

2. The results of the historical connection between Christendom and Europe today.

(*a*) Behind the idea of democracy lies the fact of the limitation of political power through the proclamation of the Gospel, the relation between the conscience and God, and the existence of the Church. Christian life thus automatically exercises an influence in the direction of constitutional limitation of the power of the state and its own association with it.

(*b*) Behind the slogan 'Freedom of the individual' lies the appeal to the individual through Christian preaching, the relation of the individual conscience to God and the resulting relativity of all other associations.

(*c*) Behind the arrogant rationalism that enabled the Europeans to colonize the earth lies the destruction of the world's gods through Christian preaching about the power of the Creator and the powerlessness of the national gods.

(*d*) Behind the revolutionary movements of our day lies the Christian preaching about the Kingdom of God, secularized into revolutionary ideologies, and the confusion of utopias turned to social criticism of the existing order.

3. Anyone who does not recognize the complex nature of the causes of the modern crisis will judge it one-sidedly either as the fault of earlier times or as inevitable fate, and so have a distorted view of our present tasks and possibilities. These causes cannot be assessed either historically, philosophically or purely economically.

Many accounts of the present crisis, especially from the Christian side, apply a moral criterion to history and measure earlier periods against an ideal, and so make them responsible for our present troubles. The cause of these troubles is then seen either in the break up of the medieval social order, or the 'loss of the mean' in the Age of Enlightenment, in the eighteenth century, or the abandonment of the 'principle of legitimacy' through the 'spirit of revolution' (Vilmar, Fr. Stahl). Such a view is theologically questionable, because in it the Christian faith is equated with the philosophical outlook and the obvious characteristics of definite periods, and it is historically questionable, because it idealizes these periods, ignoring for example the schism in the Middle Ages, and misjudges the direct causes of the ending of each period. The dispute that is raging within this field of cultural criticism, fanned by strong sectarian interests, about the dating of the beginning of this disaster—whether the 'error of the moderns' began with the

Renaissance or the Reformation or with the Age of Enlightenment or with Nietzsche or the First World War—is impossible to decide. It only serves the ego of the parties in the dispute and is moreover meaningless, because there is no going back: we can only go forwards. Every course of action in the past sooner or later becomes error to succeeding generations, which are compelled by crises to abandon it; and where else should man finish in his attempts at a purely this-worldly system, but in a series of culs-de-sac? What we need is not recrimination about the past, but an understanding of why the ideologies of our forbears turn out to be illusions to us, and to what extent they are inadequate to answer our present day questions.

4. A contribution towards the better understanding of the complex causes of our crisis has been made by the historical materialism of Karl Marx (as long as his metaphysical prejudices are ignored) because it reveals some important factors that are overlooked in a purely philosophical view.

5. Historical crises never occur just through the mysterious spread of evil, godlessness, and so on. There is always present the latent internal problem of social order, the fact that in the progress of history the existing forms become inadequate and break down. So Thomism for example inevitably led to Nominalism, medieval Christian culture led to its secularization in the Renaissance, and in the same way the alliance of Protestant Humanism and the Reformation led to the present crisis of bourgeois society. Marx quite rightly saw the crucial importance of the development of productive power. The increase in population and the invention of new economic and technical processes and financial methods bring about the replacement of the medieval commodity economy by the national state as a larger economic unit, which in turn produces modern nationalism. Later these factors lead to a demand for a free private economy and liberal individualism. Today they are developing towards the formation of still wider units, the state control of the economy with corresponding ideologies. These transitions do not proceed smoothly, but through a series of crises affecting the intellectual life also, varying in violence with the degree of

development of productive power. That is the story of the twentieth century, as foreseen by Nietzsche: 'Our social order will slowly melt away: we shall have shocks, the transposition of hills and valleys, such as have never been dreamed of.' A glance at the history of the Church reminds us that the Church has sometimes been guilty of supporting secularization, either in a semi-Christian assimilation of the Gospel to a this-worldly social order (Middle Ages) or the adaptation of its message to the standards of man as an autonomous being (Protestant Humanism). In doing so the Church has failed to make clear the uncomfortable and unique demands of the Word of God and the special nature of the Church.

6. The conflict of the Gospel with modern thought is the conflict between the Gospel and its own caricature—a secularized Gospel. This arose through modern man taking into his own hands in the name of his autonomy the promises of the Gospel and turning them into a programme within history and normalizing the commandments of the Gospel to his own requirements.

Thus the Christian hope of the Kingdom of God was secularized into an earthly goal within history, to be attained either by evolution according to the bourgeois belief in progress, or by revolution according to the utopian movement from Thomas Münzer to Lenin, and the classic combination of evolution and revolution in Marx and Engels. The humanism of the Gospel (II Tim. 2.4) was secularized, and completed this earthly eschatology with the idea of the coming life of men in dignity, freedom, law and community, as the only really human life. Marx said: 'With the dissolution of bourgeois society through the coming of socialism the "pre-history" of human society ends.' These forms of the secularization of the Gospel however were both completely powerless against the dehumanizing tendencies of the new social conditions created by technical advance. The liberal and socialist ideologies were only made possible through the preaching of the Gospel, and drew from it unconsciously their hope and the basis for their belief in the dignity of man. But by making all this dependent on man himself they got away more and more from their own sources. The binding force of their original humanism dried up and man became a victim of evolution instead of being the vaunted artificer of his destiny. Where Marx went wrong was pointed out by Nietzsche: 'Man dependent on himself is without support.' The nihilism latent in a secularized Gospel would inevitably be evident. That has happened today, with the result that not only liberalism but Marxism also has run into a fatal crisis. Marxism accused bourgeois individualism of reserving human dignity for a limited number of people and thus misrepresenting it generally, even among capitalists! As a secularized Gospel, claiming however to be a Gospel, it inevitably led to a totalitarian system of the technical mass-man, instead of giving dignity to all, in which man bartered his dignity for security and succeeded in losing both. The dignity of man is not an endowment to be assumed as a matter of course, nor something attainable only in a future order of society, but is based solely on the relation of man to God and is only maintained by resistance to the dehumanizing tendencies of social life that always tend to regard man as a means to an end. This resistance finds its ultimate unshakable foundation only in the relation of man to God through the Gospel. It is equally necessary at all times, and so no period can be glorified as though these tendencies were absent from it or had already been abolished by the existing social order. They were just as much a threat in the Middle Ages or in the subsequent bourgeois system as they are at the present time: only the form of the dehumanizing was different. Hence it is never easier or more difficult to remain a man, and so the mission of the Church, which through its proclamation binds men to God, is never greater or less, never more promising or more hopeless.

7. Thus the special mission of the Christian Church in modern Europe can—it is suggested—be described as follows:

Here in Europe, as everywhere else and at all times, it proclaims Jesus Christ as the real Lord of this world, under whose rule man finds his true place. On this mission its life as a community of the Church of Jesus Christ depends, in contrast to the world around it, and as such it acts as a restraining force on earthly powers and a resistance to dehumanizing tendencies. In this way it stands ready to defend man wherever he is being robbed of his dignity by being made just a means to an end. It shows to man in the present day crisis that he can only overcome and end this crisis by breaking with the various forms of secularized Gospel. At the same time, and for the sake of man, it fights for the maintenance of the unique freedom of expression that has been characteristic of western life since Constantine, for the existence and service of the Church.

THE PROMISE AND CRISIS OF MARXISM

1. In the crisis of bourgeois society Marxism claimed and still claims to be a theory which teaches man how to understand his destiny and shows him how to control it.

To those who were particularly exposed to the collapse of traditional ways of life, the proletariat, the intellectuals, and many young Europeans bewildered after 1945, Marxism seemed to be a theory which at the same time satisfies the intellect, gives the will an objective and the heart a promise. It did for them exactly what a religion does, throwing light upon the world and giving meaning to personal life. That is why its attraction is still so strong today, in spite of the forbidding and disappointing features of soviet development, which are dismissed as the temporary consequences of circumstances. The Marxist theory of the crisis may thus be summarized:

2. Marxist doctrine says about the destiny and possibilities of modern man that the crisis of our time is the consequence of the intolerable contradiction between increasing productive capacity and the existing conditions of production.

In a technical age productive power takes the form of collective production (factories, big enterprises, mass production). The conditions of production consist in the private ownership of the means of production and thus also the private acquisition of the collective products—conditions belonging to an earlier system of individual production. This contradiction produces a conflict of interests between the few who own and the many who do not, which becomes intolerable and prevents the full development of productive potential through restricting production, anarchy due to the impossibility of logical planning, imperialist wars between rival capitalist states with the consequent manufacture of unproductive armaments, cycles of crises due not to over production but to under-consumption by the propertyless masses, which today include also the masses of coloured and Latin-American peoples.

This view of the cause of the crisis leads to the following conclusions: In earlier times a society realizing perfect justice (a classless society) was just an ideal, the dream of so-called utopian socialists, an unrealizable idea not normative to the conditions of life and applied to society from outside. Today it is an actual possibility, a necessity, and the inevitable form of the society of the future, to be achieved through (*a*) the development of the technical potentialities of production and (*b*) the rise of class-conscious masses capable of taking action and aware of their situation and their interests—the proletariat. In its analysis of the causes of the crisis and the recognition of the proletariat as the historical agents producing the coming revolution Marxism sees the real achievement of so-called 'scientific socialism' as distinct from all sorts of utopian forms of socialism, including the Christian varieties.

From Marx to Lenin. In his reliance on the irresistible evolution of the dialectical process of history Marx did not regard revolutionary action as completely unnecessary, but the political organization of the proletariat into a party, which he himself actively promoted, was for him a subsidiary matter. For Lenin it was a determining factor in the revolution, without which the historical process itself would not achieve the abolition of the old social system. The reason for Lenin's modification lies in the then evident and historically significant refusal of his revolution by the European-American proletariat, thanks to the adaptability of capitalism and the relatively low per centage of industrial workers in Russia. The result was the introduction of a purposive 'idealistic' element into historical materialism: reliance on evolution gave way to deliberate and violent direction of the evolution towards the desired goal: the revolution as the spontaneous action of the masses gave way to revolution as the action of the 'avant garde' of the proletariat, the party leaders, i.e. a minority of professional revolutionaries. Connected with the introduction of this subjective element, which Marx played down, is the disproportionate moral pathos in Lenin's agitation. With Lenin hate replaces Marx's ridicule. In place of scepticism about the possibility of happiness perceptible in the later Marx, Lenin introduced messianism: instead of indifference to religion in Marx, who was interested only in 'historical materialism', Friedrich Engels made dialectical materialism into a substitute religion, which produced anti-religious propaganda as the duty of the party in order to encourage class consciousness among the proletariat.

With Lenin himself the combination of unrestricted will to power and ascetic devotion to the messianic idea produced a political combination of the dictatorship of the proletariat externally and the democracy of the proletariat internally. This situation was illusory and led inevitably to Stalin and the demolition of democratic controls, the extension of the unlimited and uncontrolled power of direction by the party leaders while still preserving a façade of democracy, the cynical disregard of the will of the people, the subordination of principle to means, and the adaptation of ideology to the needs of the leading clique in their struggle for the retention of power as an end in itself.

3. The claim that this theory provides not only a scientific explanation of the causes of our present situation but also a final and exhaustive account of the destiny and meaning of man today and in the future, rests on an axiomatic assumption of materialism. Because it is incapable of creating ethical obligations this theory is combined with a normative humanism derived from Christianity. The inconsistency of these two components is the internal problem of Marxist theory, that has produced a number of 'deviations'.

Marx himself was only interested in the interpretation and prognosis of the course of history, for which materialism was a prior assumption. The self-evidence of this axiom to him convinced him that he was the heir and executor of modern thinking. With it he exposed the materialistic character of modern scientific ideas since Bacon, and he regarded it as his task to purge modern thinking from all the remnants of 'theological' elements. Bourgeois idealism he regarded as the contemptible contradiction of a modern mode of thought that dared not face its own logic. He considered modern philosophy as primarily this-worldly and so materialism was no more than its obvious conclusion.

How on this basis ethical obligations (responsibility, sacrifice, human dignity) can be derived has always been a theoretically insoluble problem to Marxism. It tried to get round this in two ways:

1. There are actually no objective 'eternal' values. These are nothing but the expression of changing social interests, but there is (against Kant) the possibility of recognizing 'objective truth'. We can recognize the objective laws of evolution in nature and in history and from this derive indications for our own behaviour in so far as this can only be meaningful in harmony with those laws. So today the proletariat is the bearer of objective historical truth, since its interests demonstrably run parallel with the evident course of history. Hence the appeal to every individual to support the struggling proletariat.

2. Mechanical materialism from the French Encyclopedists to Haeckel was unable to come to terms with the uniqueness of the position of man in the cosmos, and did man an injustice by reducing him to the status of 'highest mammal'. From Hegel Marxism became dialectical, i.e. able to combine the idea of evolution with that of qualitative stages within this evolution reached by a jump from quantity to quality. Man is just such a recent qualitative stage of natural evolution. Hence the conflict with 'social Darwinism', i.e. the transference of naturalistic categories like the 'struggle for existence' or the 'survival of the fittest' to the human level, which occurs for example in fascism. Marx said: 'Communism as perfected naturalism is humanism: as perfected humanism it is naturalism.'

All this promises more than it performs. The basis of the ethical appeal remains still in the category of expediency. The question of the meaning of individual life is evaded instead of being answered: the individual is only an example of the species. Freedom, which is promised to man in the future society as the 'real outcome of the struggle between freedom and necessity, between the individual and the species', turns out to be the disappearance of the individual in the species, the loss of personality. Naturalism cannot be the basis of humanism, but destroys it. Theoretical materialism contradicts the practical idealism that Marxism demands from its adherents, and which in the period of struggle they are far from achieving, and which must necessarily lead to an attitude to life which Marxism always refuses to be identified with, namely practical materialism.

3. This inconsistency in Marxist theory is connected with the fact that in Marxism there is a hangover from the Christian view of man, which modern thinking believes can be based and maintained secularly. Through this error the Christian picture of man is inevitably distorted, less so in nineteenth century Marxism, more so in twentieth century fascism. The latter is thus essentially 'later AD' than Marxism. It is, as it were, an afterthought of history, an indication of the middle-class tie-up of the Church, that in Christian circles fascism should be looked upon as a defence against 'un-Christian' Marxism! Stalinism, as a later form of Marxism, is of course likewise involved in this distortion of the Christian view of man.

4. The question for the West is whether it recognizes in this Marxism threatening it today from the East the result of its own actions and a judgment upon itself.

It is a strange phenomenon: Christianity was born in the East, and grew up in the West. If today the West regards Marxism as a threat instead of a promise, it must recognize that it cannot resist the danger from the East without a conflict with itself.

Marxism proudly proclaims itself as the heir of the West, as the legitimate successor of the tradition of bourgeois 'enlightenment', which was betrayed by the middle class. George

Lukass said in Geneva in 1947: 'The crisis of the West is a socially conditioned crisis, the result of the reliance of the middle class on reason, progress and the potentialities of man: Marxism and Leninism are today the sole and direct heirs of this confidence.' Marxism is in fact the legitimate child of modern thinking in several ways:

(*a*) In its understanding of reality, 'real' being what is scientifically demonstrable.

(*b*) In its view of science. Everything real is scientific, i.e. demonstrable by the natural sciences: hence its reliance on science as the only legitimate interpreter of reality and as the signpost to the control of the laws of evolution in nature and in society.

(*c*) In its belief in progress. Man is progressing upwards towards the goal of a really human society: a secularized Christian eschatology.

(*d*) In its optimism. Man is by nature ready to recognize the truth and to accept his fellow man, i.e. open to truth and community, and only obstructed by external circumstances.

(*e*) In its naturalistic anthropology. Man is the product of nature, with no connection with transcendence. Mind is a later evolutionary product of nature.

(*f*) In its rationalism. Man is by nature rational, and controllable through his intelligence and by society: hence he can be organized on purely rational principles.

(*g*) In its view of the meaning of human life. The purpose of life is happiness, i.e. the highest possible development of human potentialities and the satisfaction of human needs. The individual maintains the species: that is the meaning of transcendence and hence of the individual.

(*h*) In its view of history. History is regarded from the standpoint of the natural sciences, with the dominant idea of evolution: its motive force comes from material interests and not from ethical decisions.

(*i*) In its view of Christianity. Christianity is just another religion among many, but religions are the intellectual products of a pre-scientific age.

5. Marxism claims to be scientific knowledge, but in face of the devastating criticism from science and from history can only maintain itself in so far as it has become a creed and has means of compulsion at its disposal.

Lenin proclaimed pathetically: 'Marxism is all powerful because it is true.' In fact Marxism as a system is as threadbare as an old coat, owing to criticism from the philosophical and national-economic sides, and also to the quite different course of social development from that which Marx had predicted. For this reason Marxist orthodoxy is no longer open to discussion, but has to withdraw into dogma. Thus Marxism today appears either in single elements, through which it has played a useful part in modern thought, like Plato, Hegel and others, or as a closed dogma, which tries partly to come to terms with the changed conditions, and partly withdraws from discussion behind a Chinese wall, because it dare not run such a risk.

It would however be a mistake to assert that on that account Marxism is no longer a factor to be taken seriously. However powerfully it is refuted by scientific criticism and by the course of history, these alone cannot defeat it. The power of its appeal and its present-day significance as an intellectual force are more deeply rooted than just in the apparent truth of its theoretical hypotheses:

(*a*) It serves the soviet leadership not only as a means of propaganda for mobilizing the masses and the intellectual subjugation of the conquered nations, but also (independently of the question whether it still believes in the communist 'ideals') it defines its own view of the world, which is basic to its political action, particularly its view of the non-communist world as a world inevitably in decay and yet continually determined on the destruction of the Soviet Union, and its confidence in the ultimate victory of its system. This view of the world can only be shaken by the actual proof of the vitality and efficiency of the western world.

(*b*) Marxism answers the need of the masses for something to believe in at a time when naturalism and the secular character of modern thinking have become a self-evident basic presupposition for a great part of humanity. It offers in pseudo-scientific guise a simple sort of humanism, which promises easy orientation in the world, salvation from nihilism and pessimism, and the satisfaction of material needs. This promise exercises a very powerful effect on Asiatic peoples today, after western liberalism has failed to ease their burdens. Even though among western nations the appeal of Marxism today has very much declined, through the unfavourable historical conditions, i.e. the raising of the living standards of the masses, the association of the workers in the state, and the disappointing development of the Soviet Union, yet it may at any time be revived by violent crises in the West.

6. The strong intellectual appeal that Marxism still exercises on part of the human race does not alter the fact that it is facing a mortal crisis. It is not only a product of Western thought but particularly a product of the nineteenth century. However accurate the Marxist diagnosis of capitalism was in many ways, it is none the less true that some errors in it caused a false prognosis, which is clear enough today. The evolutionary tendencies resulting from technical production do not lead to the liberation of the masses, but to the formation of totalitiarian systems with a sinister concentration of power in the hands of the leaders. The crucial question therefore concerns the nature of the opposing balancing forces which in this era make it possible for man to be man.

In the nineteenth century Marxism was not aware of this, and so in the twentieth century it has become an ideological façade for the dehumanizing of man in the whole technical set-up. The tendency to totalitarianism, which is the natural result of an outlook formed by historical materialism, does not represent an inescapable fate, as long as counter-forces are operative, that are able not to remove it but to contain it. The factors tending towards totalitarianism are not only technical production and the increase in population, but also the spiritual crisis that arose when it became clear that the naturalism and secularism of modern thinking can only lead to nihilism.

The decline in the appeal of communism in the western

nations is thus no great comfort as long as no positive belief takes its place. To the working class this decline means the loss of the great ethical impulse that was found in the socialist utopia and its powerful sense of solidarity. The result is that nihilism has a freer course and that the masses are ready to take refuge in political mysticism and are likely to follow fascist charlatans in future times of crisis.

7. Thus the dispute with Marxism must (*a*) expose the fatal crisis which Marxism faces today and because of which it cannot be the solution to the problems of our time. (*b*) It must make clear to what extent modern thinking, of which it is the most vivid expression, is condemned along with it, and that if this thinking with its inherent materialism is not overcome, the communist doctrine may gain an increasingly powerful appeal or be replaced by other no less dangerous aberrations. (*c*) It must show where man can find the kind of allegiance without which the dehumanizing tendencies of social evolution will prevail, and how through the consciousness of this allegiance these tendencies may be restrained by the state and economic organization.

Scientific criticism of Marxism is thus not sufficient by itself: it would be just as useless if an existential view of man were substituted for the naturalistic view, if irrationalism took the place of rationalism, agnosticism replaced the credulous belief in science, or if materialism were replaced by an idealism, which was unable to break through the fundamentally secular way of thinking. Modern man's hesitation between nihilism and the need for faith would not be removed in this way.

8. The Church of Jesus Christ has not got to refute Marxism philosophically before it can introduce the preaching of the Gospel: it has not got to meet it on the philosophical plane and by means of ostensibly more correct ideas to give man the personal allegiance which Marxism promised but could not really give. It has not got to persuade man to some conception of social order, but to bind him to Christ: by its testimony and life it has to present the reality of God, which was revealed in Jesus Christ as the salvation of man accomplished by God. Over

and over again in the past, not just today, man has lost his centre: beyond all our efforts it is restored to us in Christ. This Christ is Lord of history and Lord and controller of the totalitarian set-up.

The Christian community, where Christ is believed and confessed is the curb on the totalitarian state in the East and the protection of man against the dehumanizing effect of technical production in the West.

By its living presence and by its responsible influence upon the organization of public life it contributes to the limitation of the power of the state, the association of the power of the state with justice, the direction of law to the service of man, the protection of man against tyranny and exploitation, the maintenance of an area of freedom for individual responsibility, the respect for conscience and freedom of belief, and the prevention of the use of man as a means to an end.

In order to do this the Church must not wait or hope for the masses in the western nations to return to it, nor must it strive to become a political force as a means to that end. Whether it will be granted to it to provide a sufficient and effective counterforce to check the dangers which threaten us today is a question it must leave in God's hands. It must enter the lists at once without regard to the smallness of its numbers or its lack of strength, and can console itself with the thought that even in a technical age it is not quantity but quality that is decisive. If it has the courage to be a 'creative minority' God's word will not return to it void.

9. In this conviction the Church cannot remain indifferent to the efforts to create a European community.

Defence against communism is not the only problem pressing towards the unification of Europe, nor must it be the main objective. Everyone is committed to defence who believes that communism, contrary to its promise, is giving men stones instead of bread, and that the ills of our society can still be cured by other methods than that of Dr Eisenbart,[1] which communism

[1]The hero of a popular student song, celebrated for his drastic (and usually false) surgery.

offers. But to concentrate only on the question of defence is to misunderstand the task before us. The difficulty is that there are two contradictory elements involved in this task, that cannot be treated independently of each other, defence and association, prestige and co-existence. Because Europe does not end at the existing frontier of western Europe, our relationship to the nations of the communist bloc and their problems is a matter of vital importance, including the problem of communism itself which—make no mistake—is for these people by no means merely a matter of external domination, but an irrevocable turning point in their history. In Europe today we have one of the most urgent problems of humanity to solve, the relationship between the struggle of East and West for the shaping of society in the future, and positive co-existence. The Church as such is not partisan in this struggle. Its presence inevitably impinges on three points where both sides are particularly sensitive:

1. It points inexorably to the individual man of today as the focal point of this struggle, and as the direct responsibility of both the contending parties.

2. It demands from the impenitent self-righteousness of both contending parties the change of heart necessary before anything salutary can happen, even a salutary defence against communism, as the fate of the German people between 1933 and 1945 clearly warns us.

3. It stands for the old Christian truth (Augustine) that the aim of conflict is peace, reconciliation and peaceful co-existence. The struggle has a different aspect according to whether the contestants aim at the destruction of each other or peace. Thus it can be of crucial importance how the Church involves itself in what is happening between the contending parties, how it believes and lives and loves among the nations.

V

THE CHURCH IN A DIVIDED WORLD

One of a series of lectures delivered at Strassburg in April 1954

THE WORLD that the crucified Christ looked upon from Golgotha was, and still is, a divided world. The world to which he offers his outstretched arms and would hold so closely to his heart 'with its thousand sufferings and burden of indescribable sorrow' is a bundle of unruly rebellious fragments, that not only reject this invitation and this Saviour, but resist the fellowship in which they are all loved by the one Saviour and held in one embrace by the same universal love. They are all dependent on the same mercy; they are all meant to live in the house of the same Father and Lord as his children and servants—the Jew with his consecrated life together with the primitive fire-worshipper and the elegant sybaritic lawless cynic in Rome; the members of the different confessions, as though their differences were of no account; the Poles and the Germans; the French and the Germans at the time of their bitterest antagonism; the exploiter and the exploited, without regard to their differences, which seem irreconcilable; the Jews and the Germans, transcending the gas chambers and the concentration camps, that seem to separate them for ever—they are all included in the love of the same Father. From Golgotha Christ sees them all—the enmity of hostile neighbours on the same corridor of the block of flats; the discord of the parties in a broken marriage, for whom having to live together is hell instead of heaven. He sees all these rejecting a heaven, in which they should live together, enjoying the joys of friendship. He sees them prepared, in the hysteria of hate and fear and mistrust, to let themselves go up in flames with the others in the mushroom cloud of a nuclear bomb, rather than live amicably together. He sees them all and stretches out his wounded hands over them all, and holds them all close to his heart pierced for them all, and in one life and one death binds them together in unity with himself, making himself the one way, the one truth and the one life for them all, barring all other ways and condemning as lies all other truths that disrupt this unity, and exposing as a broken well all other sources of life, which pretend that there is any other way of life but in community.

But those whose eyes have been opened, who have recognized the power and truth of this unshakable and unifying love; those who see that it is senseless to resist it or to seek a basis for life elsewhere and so to maintain the barriers between man and man; those who have therefore ceased resisting and are content to be taken one with another to his heart by this Saviour and together to rely on his sacrifice and to live together by the devotion of his life—these form the Church.

When we speak of the Church in the divided world, we are proclaiming the message of this one all-embracing and unifying love. If this 'all' and this 'one' are true, then there is simply no reason for regarding any other men as outside its scope, no reason for restricting or rejecting this community, no reason for ascribing to any differences a validity and force which might in any way restrict or spiritualize or obscure this unity. Belief in the validity and force of differences would indicate at once disbelief in the validity and force of the unity wrought in Jesus Christ, and raise the question whether it is not rather I myself who am excluded from this unity, if by resisting in any given case this togetherness within the arms of the Crucified I am excluding other people as unclean 'wild beasts and creeping things and fowls of the air' (Acts 10.9-16).

But if I admit in reference to any differences in the world, differences of race, nationality, class or ideology, a power of separation greater than the unifying power of Christ, or regard this unifying power as having meaning only for heaven and not on earth, only for the life beyond and not for this life, only in God's sight and not amongst men, then I am immediately admitting that I am not living by this all-embracing love, but by standards and values relating to these differences, and that therefore the Gospel is valid may-be for eternity but certainly not for earth. I should have produced a Platonic Christianity without the Incarnation or the historical reality of the Cross, or the Resurrection or the hope of a new world as a real world—and so rejecting the whole content of the Christian creed. When Goethe in a satirical poem described the history of the Church as 'a mixture of error and violence' it was the faithlessness of the Church in just that sort of Platonizing that prompted him to do so, by which the Church encouraged the 'principalities and powers' to maintain the appearance of permanence, so that the differences dividing men were not seen to be merely relative, but were regarded as irreconcilable and even given religious sanction by a theology of creation transformed into an ideology.

The history of the Church presents a divided picture: its message was not without effect. It produced in Greco-Roman society a hitherto unheard of humanizing of the relation between masters and slaves; it modified profoundly the restriction of justice to a privileged section of mankind, the Greeks and the Romans; it provided a deeper and more effective basis for the unity of the human race than late classical ethics was capable of achieving; it is the unconscious basis of modern humanism. It is no accident that modern anti-humanist movements that deny this unity and try to substitute for it the polytheism of races, have always become instinctively anti-Christian. The Christian message has produced a consciousness of human unity that has often enough liberated men from the cohesive force of class or national groups, and made possible direct contact between separated individuals. Impressive illustrations of this are provided by the biographies of the great Christian personalities, the history of missions and also such humanitarian efforts as the Red Cross. If anyone asks what changes have taken place in the world in the last two thousand years he must be referred to the fact that the universal recognition of human dignity, the respect for it even in the person of the aboriginal Australian bushman and of the most depraved criminal cannot be accounted for in any other way than through the worldwide recognition of Jesus Christ as the 'man for all'. When Ernest Renan said that he could not believe that a Papuan could attain eternal life just like a European, he was denying Jesus Christ in the same way that Adolf Hitler did when he said, in a speech in 1933, that the difference between the highest anthropoid apes and the most primitive men was less than that between these latter and the highest developed race (the Nordic of course). Both statements reveal how little to be taken for granted and how easily lost sight of the realization of the unity of man and the universality of human dignity really is, and that the idealistic view of man distorts it just as much as the naturalistic view. As long as man does not discover in the death of Christ the truth about his own existence all the blessings and possessions that have been given him by God become in his hands means to set himself up against God and to exalt his own righteousness, and so to get rid of God: just so long do these material possessions that he is so proud of form absolute differences, and the barriers of collective groups become walls, the scaling of which is prevented by the application of all legal, police and moral means. But where the wall is scaled and man is brought face to face with man, then, even though unconsciously, the will of God is obeyed and the Gospel is shown forth.

I recall the film *Die Brücke* (The Bridge): a German woman army doctor, carried off by Jugoslav partisans, comes gradually to see this as a call. The fact that the partisans are enemies and that by healing them she is serving the military potential of the enemy becomes unimportant in comparison with the inescapable duty of healing, which is based on the realization of common humanity, against which the appeal to her national, even her comradely duty is helpless, however strong the logic of this appeal may be, since the fingers of a wounded partisan, which she is so glad to see again capable of movement, are immediately bent to shoot at her friends. The film illustrates the nature of the conflict of the Germans with their own recent past: it does not venture as far as the overt question about the justice of the war waged by the German forces against the Jugoslavs; it contents itself with hinting at this question by its sympathetic portrayal of the partisans, by the direct moral certainty that they exhibit, by the mention of a German punitive expedition against a Serbian village and the equally primitive and clearly inadequate self-justification of a German officer, who argues that because of the surrender of the regular Jugoslav army, the partisans are nothing but criminal bandits. But the timidity of the presentation of the problem does not prevent the insistence on the claims of humanity against all other laws and logic, at least for a doctor. A doctor must never simply identify himself with a party and restrict his activities within the limits of his party and its aims. For him the conflict of parties must become unimportant in comparison with his special task; he must remain above it and be influenced more by the community of suffering than by the rights and wrongs of parties. The army medical officer himself, who put forward the primitive self-justification that the partisans were bandits, expresses this equally correctly but primitively by his devoted concern for a wounded partisan prisoner, and to the question how he reconciled this with what he had previously said he answered that this had nothing to do with the case, for he was a doctor after all. A doctor is thus someone for whom parties and guilt cease to exist: there are only people suffering and in need of help—an attitude which is, as we know, all too easily lost sight of, and was often forgotten altogether during the last war and most terribly in the experiments on human beings carried out by Hitler's doctors. This attitude of mind is a consequence of the healing work of Jesus Christ for all men, and shows the Church the part it should play, which is exactly like the function attributed in this film to the doctor. Thus we can see what the Church exists for on earth and how it should behave in a divided world.

The Church cannot boast of this mission, 'that no flesh should glory' (I Cor. 1.29). Instead its task sets the standard by which the Church is judged on its course through history, and which shows up its shortcomings. The Church has indeed been faithless often enough in not condemning the disunity of the world and even in identifying itself with it, giving it religious sanction and itself providing new material for it, aggravating the division of the world into factions by the disunity of Christianity itself. It may be sufficient to remember the persistence of slavery in the Christian world as late as the nineteenth century, or the alliance of the Church with the class hierarchy, or the exacerbating effect of the different Christian confessions and their priests on the national conflicts—every Christian confession has its share of blame here—or the pogroms, massacres and funeral pyres that mark the history of the non-conforming minorities, or the annihilation of the American aborigines beneath the banner of the Cross, or the association of missions with colonialism, which has produced in our day the revolt of the coloured peoples against white hegemony, and even encouraged the hostility of coloured Christians against the white, that is not at all unfamiliar even in the ecumenical movement.

But what is meant by the 'Church' in this connection? It is easy to point to guilt and failure on someone else's part and the allusion to the guilt and failure of the Church is indeed often enough directed at some group outside our own. Where that is so, criticism is unprofitable, for this is a question of the use of criteria that can only be rightly applied where our own existence is involved, because this standard is nothing less than the all-embracing and unifying love of the Crucified Christ. No doubt the Church as an organized body is included, together with its individual representatives, its preaching, which has so often failed to present boldly and definitely enough the actual consequences of the coming of Christ, its preachers, who have often behaved like party officials, its spokesmen who have so often put obstacles in the way of the spirit of Christ instead of clearing a path for it. But the blame cannot be limited to these. Is there any one of us who is free from blame?

In November 1945 the well known caricaturist Low published a cartoon depicting an English middle-class couple at breakfast, reading in the newspaper the disturbing account of shortages in central Europe during the coming winter. They were saying: 'Why should we worry about the Germans? It serves them right!' And all round them were the spectres of refugees cold and starving, and Death unrolling a motto over them: 'Sickness knows no frontiers'. Such couples are familiar in all countries, indeed, which of us has not behaved like them at times? We can imagine them going to church on Sunday and being proud of belonging to the western Christian tradition. It is pointless to discuss with these people whether or in how far the Germans brought their fate upon themselves, and whether it is true of all or only a proportion of them. To raise the question at all is a betrayal of the Gospel and is the most serious obstacle to the admission of guilt by the Germans, that we should all like to see. What is there so profoundly un-Christian in the attitude of the couple in this cartoon of nine years ago, and which is still present with us? To think as these people do is to assume the righteousness of their own life with no need of repentance. Others may have deserved whatever misery comes to them, but they themselves are free from blame. But that is to shut out the sufferers from humanity. Nothing separates us more from one another than being right when someone else is wrong and insisting on acting accordingly. My rectitude always conjures up the danger of the most profound separation, the division into two worlds between which there is no bridge, not even the bridge of genuine sympathy and compassion. For my rectitude forces the other into the wrong, and thus provokes in him the effort to find something that he is right about, in order to force me into the same position of being wrong. Thus the conflict about being right is the bitterest and toughest existing among men and obscures the common evil into which we are driven by this alone. We can find plenty of 'motes' in the eyes of others to use to find fault with them. In doing so we lose sight of the fact that these 'motes' are all splinters from the same wood that is part of our own make-up. A member of a nation which is so burdened with shame and guilt as the Germans are runs the risk of being misunderstood, but would be failing in his duty to the others if he did not point to the universal tendency to evil: sickness knows no frontiers, including the sickness of totalitarianism, antisemitism, superstition and hysteria, paranoia and fear—none of these are specifically German evils; they can afflict any people, as can the blindness and stupidity that goes with them, and anyone who can still boast of clean hands, because the sickness is only to be found in the house next door, may well consider what blood and filth and guilt would cling to his own hands, if he happened to have been born a few kilometres further east. Sickness and evil know no frontiers and can really only be constrained by the boundless mercy upon suffering and guilty men that shines from the Cross and calls us to follow.

We asked who makes up the Church, and the quick and facile answer that we are all the Church is given point by the Low cartoon showing that the guilt and failure of the Church are our guilt and failure, particularly in that pharisaical division between clean and unclean, as we join the dance of mankind around self-righteousness, which divides the world like nothing else and sharpens the national, social and ideological conflicts by forcing others into the position of being in the wrong and identifies me with right and right with me. There is a hint here of the significance of the Reformation doctrine of justification in relation to the pacification of the world, and how profoundly and truly it reveals the real evil, the real poison, and the only way to reconciliation. Thus we have to keep asking ourselves afresh whether by our own attitude and its basis and methods we are not personally involved in the faithlessness of the Church and forgetting our baptism and hindering the healing work of grace through the forgiveness of the Cross.

And here, as in penitence we take a new look at the world from the Cross, we step outside the dance around the golden calf of self-righteousness; the conflicts and differences lose their absolute character in so far as they cease to be a question of self-justification. But this in fact raises another contradiction, which is the real conflict between the Church and the world, and which it is our task today correctly to understand, for with this the many arguments are concerned, for example about the place of the Church in the East-West conflict, its attitude to totalitarianism and communism. If this conflict is not rightly understood, then we have just the repetition of secular conflicts in clerical dress, a new form of self-identification with right and truth, which is found in all ideologies: it is thus just an ideological conflict. The real conflict arises from the fact that in recognition of the common need for forgiveness and common acceptance into the arms of the crucified Christ, the division of men into clean and unclean, the exclusion of a section of humanity, cannot any longer be accepted. In place of the creation of irreconcilable differences, the Gospel of reconciliation, the breaking down of barriers and a new irreconcilable conflict of quite another sort arises between the practice of love and the practice of hate, between exclusion and acceptance. It was a last echo of the biblical 'for all' when in 1917 the new Soviet government sent out to the world a radio broadcast with the glaring title 'To all', to announce a new era of freedom and justice. But this 'To all' only appeared to be as universal as the Gospel; in fact it was addressed not to all but only to those who were conscious of being oppressed, excluding those who were declared to be oppressors. The assumption behind it was the division which Raymond Aron (in *The Permanent War*, 1953) described as 'the manichaean view of the world' in communism: the division of the world into angels and devils, which with its 'logic of schizophrenics' must inevitably transform any war into a religious and civil war, which was the declared aim of Lenin in regard to all national conflicts. Here training in hate becomes an integral part of education, and the certainty of being in possession of the panacea for all the ills of all humanity sanctifies every means in the struggle and deprives the opponent of the right to live and makes him a fit subject for liquidation.

In the Middle Ages, when the executioner knelt before his victim to ask his forgiveness, it was a moving expression of the fact that even the death penalty as the extreme implementation of the law was not based on the identification of the human judge, or his instrument the executioner, with the law, and that it did not absolve the human judge from himself being worthy of death as a sinner. It was just a matter of duty and necessity, which only deprived the criminal of his physical life, without excluding him from the community of grace and driving him into absolute outlawry, but it commended him to the same eternal grace on which the judge himself relied. The further the modern world gets away from the influence of the Christian Gospel the more the death penalty becomes merciless elimination, the absolute denial of the right to live, as was shown most horribly in the National Socialist treatment of the Jews as vermin to be exterminated, and in Stalin's purges.

In this sense the rhetorical declaration of the First Secretary of the Georgian Communist Party after Beria's execution is revealing: 'In the name of the Georgian people threefold curses upon this monster, whose hands are dripping with the blood of hundreds of thousands of the best sons of the Soviet people, including Georgians.' The death penalty, which in the Middle Ages was a temporal atonement that did not affect eternal destiny, was now to be extended into eternity: it is an eternal curse and the denial of any sort of human solidarity. But in that very fact it implies that the one who decrees and inflicts it is incapable of penitence: by treating others as devils he inevitably sets himself up as an angel: in order to be able to carry this hypocrisy through he needs the victim as a scapegoat, on whom all the guilt can be heaped. It is not the system of which they are all part that is to blame, not the errors, crimes and negligences, but 'It is Beria's fault', 'It is the Jews' fault', but also 'It is Hitler's fault' (thus the impenitent self-justification of the Nazi fellow-travellers in Germany and abroad) and 'It is Moscow's fault', which is the stereotyped answer to the question about the reason for the present disunity of the world. But in this it is made clear that this communist manichaeism is only the logical expression of the general manichaeism, in which the real sin of men is manifested and which leads to deeper and deeper division of the world. Where he is not restrained by the Gospel, man is always inclined to invent categories in which to divide the world into angels and devils, a world in which only men are left out. The inevitable result is the debasing of humanity, increasing barbarism in methods of conflict, general hypocrisy and spreading fear.

A young and enthusiastic German communist, who was himself subsequently the victim of a purge, asked a security police officer in 1946 whether it was necessary to carry out so many and widespread arrests in the Eastern Zone. The answer he received was: 'I am surprised at your question. Don't you know that we in our country and you in yours have to wipe out all the older generation, if we want to establish communism?' The bland brutality of this answer is worth consideration. It is basically identical with the brutality of the couple in Low's cartoon and shows the not very surprising similarity between the bourgeois and the revolutionary. The crucial point is the antithesis of the 'we' and 'the whole older generation'. For anyone to talk like that is to exclude all doubt of himself and to set himself up as the arbiter of divine justice and as the bringer of salvation. But it is no longer only living men that he is dealing with and to whom he is to bring salvation, for this is intended for those yet to come, whom he will create: he is the creator, the better creator of a better humanity. His attitude to the people living at present is that of a judge, sorting out those that are useful material for him from those that he considers useless, and which are therefore to be destroyed. At best no one is promised that he can be more than useful material, and that is how youth and the proletariat find themselves treated. As the creator-saviour he has no real counterpart: everyone but himself is just material, to which he can permit no personal relationship, only a purely objective one. But even this reacts on himself: in this depersonalized atmosphere his own personality suffocates; he becomes a cold functional mechanism, such as was produced by the SS and the Security Police.

We cannot go further into this question as to how far this depersonalization of men in the name of messianic salvation can be carried, and what prospect there is of transforming not only individuals but a whole nation and a whole generation into automatic units of a termite state. We have nowadays more evidence than in the past of the possibilities and also the limitations of this experiment, and at the same time we have as much grounds for apprehension as for hope.

What is vitally important is that we can only meet this phenomenon effectively if we are clear in our own minds firstly that it is not due solely to the manichaeism of the communist ideology, so that we are safe from it elsewhere and outside the communist area, but that the possibility of its appearance is present everywhere and is increased to an extraordinary degree by the living conditions of the twentieth century. It lurks behind every mask, every ideology, revolutionary or conservative, military and socialist, Christian and atheistic. Then secondly we must realize that to resist it we need a belief in mankind, in the indestructibility of humanity and the possibility of awakening human instincts—all of which mere humanism cannot provide and which must be based on something deeper. Nothing less than belief in the Holy Spirit is necessary for us to be able to meet the functional automaton at a human level and so to awaken the humanity in him. This is the saving and releasing element in the climate of fear and suspicion created by the messianism of the revolutionary and the pharisaism of the bourgeois and the inertia of self-righteous hearts. It is to this task that the Christian is called today. That is what the Church, including its official representatives, must stand for, boldly stepping over the apparently absolute barriers. The Church and the individual Christian can laugh at the gods to whom countless human sacrifices are being offered. Instead of anger and condemnation the Christian can appeal to the other man with unconstrained frankness through his reason, that he has long since sacrificed to his dogma, and through his free will, which he has long since exchanged for blind obedience—not relying on reason or freedom as though they were permanent and dependable human qualities (we know from bitter experience that this is not so), but rather trusting in the Holy Spirit who can set men free for intelligent understanding of reality and for free and responsible decision.

But we should be evading a problem laid upon us, we should

be misusing the work of personal ministry as a by-pass, if we confined ourselves to immediate personal contacts. The Church's task of charity and reconciliation in the divided world and the conflict which this involves with every form of totalitarian manichaeism, eastern or western, has political consequences. Because of its mission the Church is not, and never can be, identified with a party, if it really is a church. Because of this conflict it can and must sometimes and in certain cases also be ready to support a party. It cannot regard the various political decisions as being taken in a night when all cats are grey (K. Barth); it will have to make choices through its members, approving or rejecting, and to urge and guide its members to that end. The basic principle of this guidance is to be found in the Church's message. It will not be able to advocate or support any political system in which this pharisaism or messianism is elevated into a principle. And so in the twentieth century, in a limited area of political possibilities that are open to discussion, it will regard itself as responsible for the maintenance of democratic rights and liberties, because these possibilities represent personal responsibility; it will oppose the brutality and the illusions of the totalitarian pretensions to the position of creator, and it will impress upon government and citizen the duty to defend the constitutional state nationally and internationally. It will be conservative towards ideological messianism and a disturbing force in relation to ideological conservatism, criticizing the existing situation in favour of greater justice. It will not wait until the right conditions develop, but will seek to create these in every situation.

This occasional taking sides does not imply permanent and complete support for a particular party. It means that the Church sees the dangers not only from the front but also from the rear, and so realizes that the threat does not come from one side only. It will include in its concern also those with whom it disagrees and against whom it is obliged to give warning, and finally it means also that it exists and can exist as a community in every camp 'seeking the peace of the city' according to the counsel of the prophet Jeremiah. By the very fact of its existence and its responsibility in the different camps in the national and ideological conflicts of the modern world, transcending all barriers as the one brotherhood of the *Una Sancta*, the one flock of the one shepherd, it is already in fact a protest against the development of barriers into walls and iron curtains, and the Church not only has to maintain this protest against the domination and the polytheism of the collective social order and to believe in the unity of the world in the love of God, but it has also the duty to proclaim this and to be an example of it.

The crucial test of the brotherhood of the Church will always be that its members are on the one hand freed from the social groupings resulting from nature and history, as *eklektoi*, sojourners, pilgrims and strangers, bound together into a new people, and yet at the same time they are placed in this old and alien society, sharing responsibility for its life and thus also inevitably involved in its rivalries. The order of events cannot be reversed: first we are released; we are no longer just functionaries of our national interests; we are free from class allegiance; we are not primarily French and German, white and coloured. 'We are not debtors to the flesh' (Rom. 8.12) means also that we are not bound by the interests of our nation and our class and party: we stand above all such groupings. In the brotherhood of the Church we can believe and hope and trust each other to be able freely and independently to see and examine the problems arising between the nations, and should remind each other continually of these possibilities, and so address each other firstly as members of the one new people of God and only then as members of our ancient nations. That is what the new ecumenical movement is teaching us today.

This release, however, makes possible a new free and true community, without which it is not properly understood. For it does not mean at all a withdrawal, a flight from the world, but it allows and makes possible and indeed demands that we take part in the life of the world—but in a new and freer way. The Christian's involvement in the life of his nation is not caused by nature, but in obedience to his Lord: it is a mission from the

Lord exactly in the same sense as this Lord can send him forth from his native land and his friends as in the case of Abraham. Sent back again into the life of the world, the Christian now obeys his Master and not his nation. But this obedience will always take the form of responsible care for the interests of his nation. In this obedience the Christian becomes the faithful advocate of his people in the circle of the other nations. As he bears the burdens of the other nations so he will ask them to help him bear the burdens of his own nation, and so to keep in mind the interests, needs, historical heritage, internal difficulties of his people. He is permitted to love his people with all the endowments that God has lent to them, and all their weaknesses and all the difficulties that they have brought upon themselves through their own fault. His advocacy can then go as far as to involve him in the conflicts of his people, when within the narrow earthly limits the competing national interests come to blows. That is a possibility but is not necessarily bound to happen, since his loyalty to his people can very well take the form of opposition and non-co-operation. As long as his attitude derives from his release and his belonging to the body of Christ, as long as he regards himself as the ambassador of the crucified Lord, who has taken the whole world to his heart, as long as he does not wish himself or wish his compatriots to be the only ones included in the love of Christ, but shares this love with the other nations, people who differ from him in ideas and beliefs, with the godless and the self-righteous, the communists and the fascists, the manichaeans and the pharisees, as long as he is concerned that even in this advocacy and even in his participation in the hard conflicts of the world he is an ambassador for peace and spreads an atmosphere of peace around him.

VI

WAR AND THE CHRISTIAN LIFE IN OUR GENERATION

in 'Durchkreuzter Hass' (Frustrated Hate) from The Adventure of Peace, *Berlin* 1961

I

AT THE 'Bergli', the hospitable country house of the Pestalozzi family by the Lake of Zürich, the principal subject of discussion was the war facing us, when we spent the first week of August together in 1939. In the mornings Günther Dehn and Ernst Wolf gave us expositions of New Testament passages dealing with the relation between Church and State, and Karl Barth disquieted us for the first time with his views on baptism and particularly infant baptism, but behind all the special subjects there was always one that time and again became the main theme: the war that already seemed inevitable, and which would shortly divide us and put us into opposite camps. There was no possibility in our minds that this war would be able to destroy our close mutual friendship, particularly as this time there were no partisan issues to create opposition between us as was the case in former wars. For this time there was no question in our minds as to where the blame for this war lay, or how necessary resistance to Hitler's blackmail was, and consequently for which side we should wish a—we hoped—speedy victory. The presence of Pierre Maury, a short visit from Visser 't Hooft, and the discussion between the Swiss Karl Barth, Arthur Frey and Rudolf Pestalozzi about whether the obligations of neutrality implied that in the event of a possible attempt by the French to penetrate the West wall from the South by marching through Switzerland, Switzerland should take the distasteful step of taking sides with the Germans and so supporting tyranny against freedom. All these things contributed to push these most urgent matters to the front. What ought the Church in our respective countries to say in this situation? What ought the Christians on either side to do when the great massacre began, of the actual extent of which we had no idea at that time? Karl Barth demanded that the German ecumenical organs should declare to the Christians in Germany that this was a war of aggression deliberately brought about by the National Socialist leaders, and was consequently an 'unjust' war, and therefore the Christians in Germany should refuse to be called to the colours. Although we agreed with his judgment in theory, Barth found no support in our circle for this demand. We raised objections which seemed to be subsequently much too specious: the ecumenical movement would itself thereby become a party instead of standing above the contending parties: it would be impossible to make such a demand credible as an evangelical pronouncement and to keep it clear of the suspicion of political bias: the Confessing Church in Germany, which was in any case involved in a difficult struggle, would be faced with the disastrous alternative either of being persecuted as traitors to their country or of having to stand out against the pronouncement of the ecumenical movement.

Pierre Maury, who was a French reserve officer, and we Germans would perhaps soon be members of opposing armies. An ecumenical pronouncement such as Barth demanded would have applied exactly to our own situation—but both sides refused to support it for the sake of freedom of judgment, or from fear of all sorts of consequences which we wanted to spare our German brethren, and from fear of the legal misconstruction of such a pronouncement, perhaps also simply because such a step was too unprecedented, too novel, too bold. Christian theology had of course worked out a distinction between 'just' and 'unjust' wars, because for partly valid reasons it thought so to avoid a 'no' on principle to any war at all. But the effect on the Christian Church had mostly been to make pacificism a heresy and to evade the objections to participation in war. At best the distinction contributed occasionally to dissuading a conscientious prince from some warlike adventure. The promise that this distinction implied remained unfulfilled. It meant: we, the theologians, the prophets, the official spokesmen of the Church will exhort every individual to examine critically in the light of our Christian standards the circumstances of every outbreak of war, and only consent to participate in it if the result of that examination is positive, or at least not clearly negative. And further we will ourselves undertake such an examination, and if the result is negative we will make a fraternal appeal to the nation, and in any case to the Christians within it, not to participate in unjust violence. That has virtually never happened, although such a use of this distinction could have been made, and such an appeal justified, as was constantly done in dealing with the Christian pacifist groups. Because it had never happened we did not dare to agree with Barth at the time. We shied away from the unusual and forbore to put into words what we nevertheless clearly recognized. The shortcomings of the ancestors hamper the decisions of the grandchildren. That is true also of our own serious omissions during the years since 1945. The distinction between 'just' and 'unjust' wars had already become invalid before it was completely outdated by the invention of the means of mass destruction. We have no longer any right to appeal to it, because we have made use of it in the past, as long as, and in so far as it was in our favour, and because we have ignored it in our generation when we were faced with a clear case of an unjust war. A Church that would now make use of it without any sign of penitence for having ignored it when it was inconvenient, only reveals its hardness of heart and its manipulation of the commandments of God. It cannot be surprised if the world receives its message with a yawn.

In our discussions at that time, as far as I can remember, only Karl Barth saw these consequences clearly. I tended to see the question in the light of my own personal attitude. I asked myself whether, supposing I were placed against the wall as a conscientious objector, I could die with the calm certainty that I had chosen the only possible way and not just an arbitrary one. It was clear to me that mere deduction from general principles—even from the general proposition that one must not be a soldier in a national army that is waging an unjust war—cannot provide the certainty necessary at such a time. Thus I rejected every prior commitment—'Jesus will tell me what I should do'. This answer had some justification. But today it is clear to me that it cannot be any argument against the duty of the Christian Church to give guidance and advice to its individual members, or against its public confession of the understanding of the divine command, nor against the brotherly and urgent appeals of others.

II

In the early summer of 1940, around Whitsun, I received my calling-up papers. The young minister of the Confessing Church in Dahlem was to become a recruit in the motorized signals battalion at Eberswalde. Some well-disposed general moved behind the scenes and the call-up notice was rescinded. Shortly afterwards the police raided the Grüber offices and Heinrich Grüber and Werner Sylten were arrested. The extent of the bureau's activities came out in a series of trials. In September 1940 I was ordered by the police to leave Berlin. Now my military friends thought it opportune to provide me with the protection of a military uniform, and arranged for me to be called up again. On December 5th the doors of an infantry barracks in Potsdam closed behind me. In the intervening months I had had time and reason enough to think out my attitude to such an eventuality. The question of military service had often been discussed in our circles. Some of my closest friends had long since been called up and some were even high ranking officers. They all thought exactly as I did about this war and were waiting for either an opportunity to take action, such as they hoped for on July 20th 1944, or tried at least in their immediate surroundings to behave as Christians towards their comrades, subordinates, prisoners and the enemy civil population. To refuse military service and to pay for this with their lives was by their tradition unthinkable. This possibility had indeed been considered in our discussions but usually quickly brushed aside as being what seemed to be a senseless sacrifice. The impact on us of the execution of the Stettin business man, Hermann Stohr, was all the greater. I did not know him personally, but we had mutual friends. In the summer of 1940 as a Quaker he had refused the call-up and had consequently been arrested. Well meaning officers tried to save him by the offer of compromises: that he should become a clerk with reserve units or join an ambulance unit. He refused all these ways out and was eventually executed. In a last message to his friends he said he did not want the course he had taken to be regarded as the norm for everyone, but simply as a token witness against the war, to which he personally felt called by the Gospel.

This news had been constantly in my mind during these months. How far my opposite decision to obey the call-up was influenced by cowardice I cannot be sure. On the surface of my consciousness I felt free from this anyway. The deciding factor was the feeling of uncertainty that this course of action with its consequences was the one required of me and not just my own decision. I was also influenced by discussions with the 'housemother', a unique and distinguished woman, the wife of a lawyer in Offenbach. She was endowed with great spiritual gifts and had a circle of friends in the Dahlem congregation who regarded her as an inspiring and even prophetic leader. She warned us against basing obedience on reason, i.e. logical deduction of decisions from general knowledge, either with reference to the nature of this war and the National Socialist régime or from long term assessment of the future, or from consideration of the situation one might have to face in Hitler's army. She warned us against obedience 'step by step', and suggested that without any long term planning or anxiety about future problems I should accept the call-up as a dispensation from my Lord, calling me away from my congregation into another sphere of service to the men that I should meet in the army. In response to my counter-question whether it could be the Lord's will that

I should shoot other men for Hitler's sake she told me that I should come through this war without having shot at anyone—a prophecy that was in fact fulfilled. So when the call-up came I could not see in it sufficient grounds for refusal on principle, and waited to see in what situations the confessional 'No' would have to be spoken at the risk of my life.

To be sure it did seem to me necessary later on to resist the pressure to become an officer, in order not to have, apart from the private soldier's share of responsibility, the duty of defending this war before subordinates, and as soon as an opportunity arose I transferred from a machine gun crew to an ambulance unit within my company. In doing so I did not suppose that I was escaping the solid weight of guilt that rested upon my people and this army or that I could lessen my share in this guilt in any way. I did not join the ambulance unit in order to have cleaner hands than my comrades, although it might indeed not be wrong to keep oneself unspotted amidst the general slaughter, but because the service of the wounded was the only one that I could perform without prejudice against it. I was sure that in the event I should not have fired my machine gun at my fellow men, particularly in Hitler's cause, but the wounded and the sick must be looked after in any war, and so I could undertake this duty. I could not forget that this also contributed to the war, and so I could not imagine that I had in this way found an innocent means of escaping responsibility. Within the general futility I had something relatively sensible and necessary to do. That seemed to me a blessing: it clearly could not have any special merit, any 'greater righteousness' within the general evil.

To bind up wounds amidst the slaughter is surely the business of a Christian. To that extent my work as stretcher-bearer bore some relation to the Christian witness. But it is not by any means the whole witness. Thus this way out was really no solution of the problem of the Christian and war. I was a member of an army at war, enjoying its advantages in occupied enemy country, wearing Hitler's uniform, regarded by French citizens, Russian peasants and Czech work-people as Hitler's instrument for their oppression, and I had indeed taken an oath about this. I had got round the obstacle of attestation to some extent by explaining beforehand to my captain in an interview that I had requested that I could not take this oath literally and unconditionally, but only with the proviso that in the event of being required to transgress the commandments of God I should refuse obedience. This he accepted sympathetically and without reporting it further. Besides at the first opportunity I intended to transfer to the ambulance unit as being the only activity in which I could fulfil my oath. That was not a complete solution, which did not leave a host of questions unanswered and which could be recommended generally, but it was one course which was not barred to me by a definite command of God, although I was always conscious of its uncertainty. In retrospect I can only regard it as a very inadequate course, but in the light of my knowledge at the time as a possible way of obedience.

III

There is always an element of self-justification in recounting one's experiences and decisions. Consequently there is a great deal about myself in what I have written. Moreover no close examination and analysis is needed to see that it is concerned with the behaviour of a man in a period of transition: the traditional codes and conventions are no longer completely relevant, only in part. That is what is so confusing: it is not completely clear where the line should be drawn: the new rules have not yet been worked out and so the individual is left to find his own way. Rules and conventions resulting from common experience are not there in order to relieve the individual of the necessity for decision, but to help him decide by prior clarification and testing, and by the support of the community. The advice which the community of the Church was able to give to the individual at that time was completely out-of-date. The question is whether in the meantime we have caught up with and overtaken the present. This is something the Church can and must do.

Today we have to recognize that the attitude of the Church to war is not an isolated philosophical question confined to theoretical Christian ethics, a subject of specialized interest to a few individuals, like for example certain precise problems of medical ethics. War occupies a dominant place in national and social life, or at least it has done so up till now, so that the abolition of war as a means of policy that has become so essential today, marks the greatest possible revolution in national life, having a profound effect on the life of every individual, on education, on expectation of life, on personal obligations and social morality. Thus the attitude to war is the pivot in the relations of Church and State, the test of the understanding of the Christian mission, the crossroads for the relations of Christians and the world. It is astonishing that even today many theologians still think that they can pronounce on these questions without making up their minds about nuclear warfare. By this sort of thinking they have already made a far reaching decision. They have ignored the ultimatum to Christianity presented by the existence of nuclear weapons and instead have decided to go on as if nothing had happened.

The traditional debate between Christian pacifist groups and the churches has been ended by nuclear weapons, but not settled. It is ended in so far as they all have to say 'No' just as the so-called 'historic church of peace' has already said 'No' to war in its earlier forms. The churches in our country indeed are trying hard not to see this, for reasons that need closer analysis and the result of which, from a Christian standpoint, would be shameful. At the Synod of the German Evangelical Church in 1960 it was stated officially that the churches had said all that was necessary on the question of nuclear war, but unfortunately the politicians had not listened. But that is not true. Little has been said, and that little has not been sustained, and now the churches claim the credit of having said all that was necessary. By neglecting to say what was necessary the Church has a full measure of responsibility for the negligence of the politicians. These latter have never had to face an outcry from Christians, making clear beyond all doubt the evil of nuclear war. The Church has not proclaimed to them with one voice publicly and frankly and urgently that these 'weapons' are not weapons through which God can be served, that to carry out the threats with which the nations are now facing each other is a sinful rejection by the State of its God-given task, and that even the threat of such action undermines national and international life. Instead of denouncing this development of earlier methods of warfare loudly and clearly the Christian churches in our country have hesitated and stammered. Instead of proclaiming insistently the promise of God's commands they have set up endless commissions in order not to obstruct their members in the so-called Christian parties in the use of these means of mass destruction in the political tug-of-war. In this way they have contributed to the process of conditioning us to the presence of these weapons and thereby increasing their danger. They have given fresh encouragement to non-Christians not to expect from the Christian Church the sort of action and progress that would correspond even remotely with the revolutionary words of the New Testament. As hardness of heart is so often to be found amongst those who preach penitence, the churches find it hard to understand that the rejection and persecution that they meet with from non-Christians is the expression of disappointment and disillusionment arising from the shortcomings of the churches, their organs, their clergy and their official spokesmen. It is not the business of the Church, as a clever bishop recently suggested that it was, in a statement on nuclear war (no doubt knowing full well that he was offering a hopeless suggestion), to consider how in a world where nuclear weapons exist and the pre-atomic rules of politics are retained, the politicians can come to terms with the Christian 'No' to nuclear war. The churches have to pronounce this 'No' because it is God's command, thus making clear to the politicians their task, implicit in it, of pursuing their politics without war in an atomic age. This is one of those cases where reason and the command of God coincide. If the Church sticks to its last, without interfering in affairs outside its competence, it is also doing the best for the triumph of reason. Thus the old dispute about the ethics of war is ended: all Christians, if they heed the word of God, cannot do other than assert that they cannot take any part in a nuclear war, and that the employment of nuclear weapons is a misuse of God's creation. 'Whatsoever ye do in word or deed do all in the name of the Lord Jesus, giving thanks to God and the Father by him' (Col. 3.17).

In this apostolic exhortation participation in a nuclear war has no place. Applying this one clear principle to present-day world problems, to the German problems, to the position of the Church in society, to the dispute between East and West and to the problem of communism will lead step by step to a new understanding of the Christian faith and also to a compelling political insight that will conflict with much that is represented as Christian politics. The insight into the incompatibility of nuclear weapons with Colossians 3.17 is seen to be a crossroads for the whole relationship of the Christian to the world.

That old esoteric discussion among Christians about the ethics of war is ended but not decided. The position that the leading churches have to adopt, at least in the case of nuclear war, the 'peace churches' have long since accepted for war generally: participation in war cannot be reconciled with the exhortation in Colossians 3.17. In this old conflict powerful arguments were advanced by both sides. Perhaps the old slogan of 'parity' once had some justification, but not in the present dispute about nuclear arms. The ethics of war maintained by the major churches rested essentially on the distinction between 'just' and 'unjust' wars. With this it stood or fell. Today it is possible to come across theologians who calmly accept that this distinction is outmoded without however drawing the only possible conclusion from this. That is complete cynicism. The fact that the distinction is outmoded can only mean that there are no longer any 'just' wars, i.e. wars participation in which can be reconciled with the will of God, and certainly not nuclear wars. To abandon this distinction without drawing the logical consequence is to ignore the question of God's will altogether and to admit participation in all wars without distinction. The result is to act cynically or in a cowardly way instead of obediently, and to sink below the level of the old ethic of war, while claiming to be above it.

This distinction arose because men did not want to ignore the will of God, but to urge the individual to obey it. Whether it was any use is another question. At any rate, it was an attempt to make clear that there was a distinction, and that one should not participate in every war or in every aspect of it. To that extent this distinction was an attempt, in a world which it was impossible to imagine without war, to do a good Christian act by civilizing war. In doing this it could be argued that it was a greater and more effective labour of love than a flat refusal of co-operation would be. It can be said therefore in criticism of the Christian ethics of war that its failure consisted less in its formulation than in the fact that it was seldom put into practice. Just as the eulogy of temperance instead of abstinence can be a useful mask for the alcoholic, so the Christian ethics of war served rather to quieten the conscience. Has it contributed more to the civilizing of war than to its justification? In one of the principal daily papers a reporter from Eastern Asia recently wrote that the people of Laos were unsuitable for waging a real war because their Buddhist religion had so deeply impressed upon them the command: 'Thou shalt not kill', that they had become one of the most peaceful people on earth. On the other hand, Pierre Bayle once said that the impotence of Christianity showed itself in its unchanging warlike character. Was he right? Or was Heinrich Heine right when he said that only when the magic power of the Cross had disappeared would the old spirit of destruction break forth again—thus ascribing to the message of the Cross a restraining power over the spirit of war? We must not condemn our fathers because they came to terms with war too easily for our modern insights. Their restraining work was a great achievement, never completed but yet undertaken again and again with great earnestness and not without a measure of success. Technical advances made nonsense of these attempts. Warfare has broken through the restrictions which pre-Christian custom and Christian ethics had laboriously imposed, and has reverted to the undisguised, unrestrained, murderous brutality, that it has in essence always been. Our fathers' aim to civilize war can now only be paralleled by efforts to abolish it altogether, pursued with the same earnestness and the same devotion of hard thinking, carrying on the work of our fathers with the knowledge that the old Christian ethics of war was not impracticable, as is often said today, but in its application shows that there cannot be a 'just' nuclear war and that this is in fact a contradiction in terms. That is obviously only a negative judgment, in reality every negative statement concerning war involves a positive proposition concerning peace, its nature and the conditions that make it possible. A few groups of Christian pacifists and a few Christians have advanced ahead of the churches here and discovered new territory.

All this takes time to become generally understood of course and so we must have patience with the stragglers who have not yet noticed what time it is. When I returned home from captivity in Russia I knew of course that the atom bomb existed. In August 1945 the young Jewish doctor in our P.O.W. camp at Briensk showed me a copy of *Pravda* containing on the second page a brief notice of the bombing of Hiroshima. This understatement in the Soviet press could not prevent people thinking hard about the new bomb, but I did not yet realize that it marked a caesura in history. After my return I heard my friends Hans Iwand, Martin Niemöller and Heinrich Vogel saying, like voices crying in the wilderness, that with the bomb the relative, conditional and limited 'Yes' that the Church had said hitherto to war was at an end. I did not see this and brought forward against them all the arguments that I have heard *ad nauseam* since I came to agree with them. We are in a period of transition. Understanding grows slowly, but we have not much time. For that reason it is a disaster that the Church should limp behind instead of taking the lead and by its leadership helping to build the new morality relevant to the atomic age and its dangers. In our country an attempt is being made by the authorities to ensure that the people realize as little as possible about the situation and its perils. Church circles are allied with these political interests, and glad that the excitement about the question of nuclear weapons is dying down and the Synods can turn again undisturbed to the 'real concerns of the Church'. But these 'real concerns' are a form of escapism when they are put in place of the supposedly 'political' questions instead of being considered in connection with them. It is impossible to discuss the Holy Communion today without deciding about nuclear war. It is impossible today to believe in and proclaim the reconciliation of God and men at the Cross of Calvary without recognizing the threat of nuclear war for what it is—rebellion against the reality of the atonement. The 'Yes' to the Gospel and the 'No' to war today must go together —or both will be lost.

VII

THE CHRISTIAN CHURCH AND COMMUNIST ATHEISM

Synopsis of a lecture on 'Marxism and Christianity' delivered in the Free University of Berlin in the Winter of 1958-9

1. BY COMMUNIST atheism we understand the elevation of logical rationalism and immanentism[1] into the dogma of a social-revolutionary movement. This movement uses a particular system of interpretation of the world and at the same time supports it. In this system only such methods of observation of nature, history and human life are allowed as are limited to rationally intelligible and rationalizable elements, and only what is comprehensible within this limitation and is understood from its relation within the world is recognized as existing. At the same time it is asserted that this method of observation is completely sufficient and any other is superfluous.

2. This method of observation is an exact logical and revealing product of modern thinking and cannot be refuted without profound examination of this thinking.

3. Atheism as a dogma is made to serve a messianic revolutionary will, that sees in the claims of God an obstructive rival to the claims of man and yet itself has to overcome the intellectual vacuum of existence without God. Thus atheism is at once the postulate and the historical source of communist messianism.

4. Modern atheism, as distinct from the older form to which

[1]By this Gollwitzer means the explanation of the world from within itself.

the younger Marx looked back, grew up entirely in a cultural milieu determined by Christianity. By displacing the elements of magic and myth Christianity opened the way to a rational and immanent (i.e. scientific) interpretation of the world. Christianity is partly responsible for this atheism because of its failure to deal with the questions thus raised, and through a misguided attempt to dominate the intellectual life, and through inadequate grasp and manifestation of the import of the message entrusted to it. It has been said of this atheism and of materialism and terrorism also: 'The communists show us in fair copy what they have learned in our school' (Josef Bernhart); 'The communists are hated primarily because they have dragged the skeleton out of the secret cupboard of western culture' (William Horton[1]); 'Communism is at the same time the product of the godless West and the protest against godlessness' (Nicolas Berdyaev).

5. Communism will maintain atheism as its official dogma as long as it remains messianic. In origin communism is primarily a socio-revolutionary movement and only secondarily philosophical. The reversal of this order has been due to psychological and historical reasons in operation from time to time and has been corrected again and again. The question whether atheism is an essential part of communism must be transferred from aristotelian-universal concepts (material-accidental) into historical categories. Messianism is in complete and utter opposition to the Christian faith. The combination of messianism and social revolutionary programme had a historic origin and can be defeated historically. Moreover, as M. Reding rightly says, the atheistic thesis is not the logical consequence of dialectical and historical materialism, but is a metaphysical addition: materialism itself could also be understood simply as a system of interpretation of the world 'from below'. The factors tending to weaken and ultimately to break up this combination are the sobering effect of the gradual realization of the social revolution, the influence of old and new social conditions, the experience

[1] *Christianity, Communism and History*, Nashville, 1954.

of the immutability of human nature and the insoluble and unchangeable uncertainties of human life. The first result of this development is that there are already Marxists and Marxist groups today that are uninterested in the metaphysical dogma of atheism.

6. In overcoming messianism it is not a question of disillusionment, that replaces utopianism by scepticism, but of disillusionment about man himself, that transforms an abstract humanism into a concrete form: then present-day man is no longer sacrificed to an imagined picture of humanity in the future, but the revolutionary energies become productive in the service of man as the object of the love of God and of a 'real utopia' (Walter Dirks).

7. The Christian community is one of the social factors influencing communism. Experience of the un-Christlikeness of the Church has contributed to communist messianism, and so by showing herself more Christlike the Church could contribute to its rejection.

8. The Christian Church may therefore pray and hope that the spirit of her Lord may change the fanatical rejection of God, to whom she has so often borne such inadequate witness, into a new understanding that may lead from a doctrinaire to a concrete humanism. She can only hope to be the instrument of this transformation, if she does not refuse the penitence, to which the communist accusation calls her.

9. Among the truer forms of witness that the Christian community must offer are:

(*a*) Evidence of profound penitence, which is concerned not only with the shortcomings of earlier generation but still more of our own.

(*b*) Detachment from all false associations opposing communist atheism. While the western churches expect of the eastern that they should distinguish carefully between the Church's message of peace and eastern peace propaganda, they themselves have not worried much about keeping Christian opposition to communism free from other forms of anti-communist propaganda with quite different motives, and so have allowed the Christian protest to become a weapon in the cold war.

(*c*) A new joyous and assured devotion to their Christian faith, demonstrated by willingness to suffer. This would refute the communist expectation that as the result of anti-religious agitation and administrative chicanery Christianity will reveal itself as mere convention and rapidly die away.

(*d*) Support for efforts aimed at removing the conditions 'in which man is a humiliated, enslaved, forlorn, contemptible creature' (Marx).

10. The Christian community must regard the abolition of the traditional rights of the Church by the communists as the judgment imposed by her Lord on her shortcomings and her distortion of the Gospel, and also as a mission into a new and still unfamiliar country. She will therefore have to refrain from natural and tempting indignation and self-pity. She cannot regard the outward reconciliation between the Gospel and the world, under which she has lived for fifteen hundred years, as a condition to which she has a right and on which she could depend, nor can she therefore protest and complain if it comes to an end. She will have to accept the new situation as a challenge and believe in the power of her message to carry out her mission, just as in the early days of Christianity.

11. The present conflict between West and East cannot be identified with the conflict between the Gospel and atheism. The Gospel, as news of the reality of the living God, has just as much difficulty with us in the West as with those in the East; it is just as alien and just as close, and resists all our attempts to render it innocuous (in the West by strangulation and in the East by neglect).

12. Christianity in the non-communist world, particularly in the so-called Christian countries, offers a general picture of impenitence. The alliance for the defence against the communist threat is a temptation to ideologize the Gospel, to self-justification, pharisaical division into black and white, and in many ways confirms the thesis of historical Marxism about the 'class-bound nature' of the Christian religion. The real support that

western Christianity in its outwardly easier situation can give to the eastern churches consists in encouraging the same freedom of criticism of their own social system and its ideologies and pharisaism that is expected from the Christians in the East and which has to be shown by them every day.

13. The Church in the communist world survives, humanly speaking, firstly thanks to the period of tolerance that is possible in the communist state by reason of the theory that religion will die out in a socialist society, and, secondly, in spite of the opposition that the state considers necessary because of the Marxist thesis of the danger of religion in a socialist state. The Church lives in an unstable, insecure position, in an atmosphere of vacillation between tolerance and opposition and in fear of what might happen. She must regard this thankfully as evidence of the fundamental insecurity of her life in the world, and as a call to seek her security in her Lord and nowhere else, and as a new test of her faith.

14. The Church has not only to accept the fact that she lives in a world no longer Christian, but to accept and affirm this as a dispensation from her Lord. Her efforts therefore must not be dissipated in hoping without justification for some external action to end communist domination, but instead she must make her own positive contribution within the society in which she is placed. She must not hope to get rid of communism (which would be not only illusory but internally enervating) but help to make of it something useful for the people living under it.

15. The Church's proper social contribution is always along the lines of humanizing society, the maintenance and improvement of justice, and the establishment of areas of freedom as spheres of individual responsibility. In a constitutional state the Church will feel a share of responsibility for upholding justice and freedom, for the control and limitation of all forms of human power: in a totalitarian society she will direct her responsibility towards winning these advantages and for the gradual whittling away of totalitarianism.

16. The Church in the Communist state makes her contribu-

tion to changing the communist system, i.e. the ending of totalitarianism:

(*a*) by her independent existence, her congregational life, her services and her message. Thus within the sphere of the Church the gods of this society are not recognized and worshipped as gods, and life is lived under the grace and law of the living God.

(*b*) by participating, as an organization as well as individual members, in society: by taking part in the building up of society, while at the same time refusing to worship its official gods, thus preserving always a distinction between socialist practice, in which she participates, and the messianism, which she denies. In this way she contributes towards the dissociation of atheism from socialism. As long and in so far as the communist state accepts this limited loyalty on the part of Christians, it admits willingly or unwillingly the possibility of this dissociation.

17. There are hopeful signs that such a dissociation might be achieved in the course of time:

(*a*) The sobering effect of working on the creation of the socialist state.

(*b*) The discovery that the burdens and problems of human nature do not change.

(*c*) The inner conflict between the assumption that Marxism is a rational and historical mode of thought based on empiricism on the one hand, and the messianic claims to absolute authority on the other.

(*d*) The contradiction between the aim of promoting human freedom on the one hand and the concentration of power over mind and material on the other. Unlike the case of National Socialism, this totalitarian concentration of power in communism is not in theory an end in itself, but a temporary means to an end.

18. The discarding of atheism as a dogma, that is perhaps possible in the future development of communism, would considerably ease the position of the Church in communist countries, but would presumably bring about new and different

temptations. For instance, supposing that the communists should hit upon the idea of doing what they had hitherto obstinately refused to do, and had accused the other side of doing, namely the idea of using Christianity as an ideological façade, and in addition of offering the Church an alliance—a new version of earlier alliances in the history of the Church.

19. According to the usual way of thinking by both Christians and Marxists the conflict is between religion in any form and atheism. Hence the popularity of the idea of a united front of all Christian confessions or of all religions generally and all religious people against atheistic communism, understood on the basis of the central truths of Christianity. What is really in question is the conflict between religion as organized by man and the Gospel, between all possible theistic and atheistic religions of self-redemption and the life stemming from the sacrificial love of the living, forgiving God. From a Christian standpoint, therefore, atheism cannot be regarded as specially reprehensible, but only as one of the countless forms of human disbelief in the living God, upon which in the Gospel the love of God is brought to bear. Human 'fronts' are legal and pharisaical. The Gospel means an end to 'fronts' and releases the individual from them. There can never be a genuine Christian 'front' against atheism. Instead Christians, as messengers of this divine intervention, are sent forth to the communists as to all other men, to proclaim a clear 'No' to the messianism of self-deliverance, but also God's 'Yes' to the atheist as a creature loved and sought by God.

20. All religions, including the Christian religion, i.e. empirical Christianity, is much more problematical from the point of view of the Gospel than from that of Marxist criticism. Consequently it is possible to discuss impartially with communists the psychological, sociological and moral problems of religion:

(*a*) It is possible to admit what Marxist criticism of religion pertinently says about the religious life being socially conditioned throughout its history, and about the continual subservience of the religious life to other interests.

(*b*) Against the antiquated insufficiency and shallowness of Marxist criticism of religion one can point to the profound depth of the religious life, the variety and depth of the impulses to religious creativity, and also the vitality and indestructibility of religion, that makes nonsense of the Marxist expectation that it will 'die out'.

(*c*) Thus the Christian faith, contrary to the Marxist verdict on religion, demands a more profound study of religions and the human experiences, needs and questions involved in them, and demands respect for the religious life. On the other hand it agrees with much Marxist criticism with respect to the inhuman distortion in the course of the history of religion and the Church.

21. Contrary to the opinion of the Marxist classics and many apologists of Christianity, the Christian faith is as little bound up with religion as with idealistic metaphysics. Religion is neither a special case of idealism nor vice versa, nor is the Christian faith a special case of both these two.

22. Besides the change in protestant theology in the last thirty years and the appearance of the philosophy of Martin Heidegger, Marxism in its own way draws its conclusion from the social-intellectual process that Walter Dilthey called 'the end of antique-Christian metaphysics'. The special vigour of its attack provides an urgent incentive to Christian thinking to face the task—not yet by any means completed—of clearing up and reformulation.

23. A most important part of this process is the recognition of the weakness of a good deal of Christian apologetics, such as the attempts to prove the creation of the world by appealing to the law of causation, or to demonstrate by reference to the actual and theoretical limits of knowledge the necessity for the idea of God for the explanation of the world. All this is taken into account today by the defenders of Diamat and in the process his lack of accuracy becomes obvious. Christian thinking should no longer contend against these positions, in which there is an *a priori* misunderstanding, but should realize that

it has not got to defend the idea of God as a stop-gap hypothesis, but to proclaim the revelation of the living God.

24. Marxist 'materialism' is a powerful reminder to a Christian theology inclining to idealism and individualism of the social dimension, the relation to history and the corporeality of human existence, as against an isolated contemplation of the 'I', against idealistic dualism and against overstressing the significance of a parade of standards. While 'materialistic' thinking aims at achieving social change from below upwards, in contrast to idealistic efforts in the opposite direction, it comes up against the Christian understanding of the sterility of mere law, and of man as a living entity of body and soul, of goodness and the significance of material reality as the creation of God (cf. the creation stories in Gen. 1 and 2).

25. Because it is not materialism as such that produces the conflict between communism and the Christian faith, but messianism and the consequent ideologizing of materialism into a closed system of atheistic metaphysics, the criticism of communism from the Christian angle is not that it is too materialistic but too idealistic, not too rationalistic but not rational enough. In protest against this ideologizing the Christian believes in taking really seriously the material nature of man and the historical background of his thinking, in the free use of reason and the empirical verification of theories about the world.

26. The free use of reason and unrestricted self-critical and self-verifying scientific work is endangered when it is made subservient to faith, but also when it is in competition with it. (Faith does not restrict reason, but opens the way for what is peculiar to it.) The expectation of the Age of Enlightenment that science would oust religion and become a substitute for it arose from a misunderstanding both of science and the Christian religion. With the removal of this misunderstanding and its consequent false antithesis the Christian is freed for unrestricted investigation of the world. On the other hand, where thinking is still dominated by the idea of competition and annihilation, more is expected of science than it can provide. The consequence

of this extravagant demand is that science loses its freedom to provide what it can. The transition from methodical to dogmatic materialism means the subjection of science (and so of all intellectual life) to the claims of the arrogant ideological requirements of faith, instead of the former subjection of science to the patronage of the Church.

27. Since it stands for the free use of reason against dogmatic rationalism, for the material world as the product of creation against dogmatic materialism, Christian thinking can recognize and come to terms with the limitations placed on human reason and thus on its understanding of and control of the world, the fragmentary nature of all knowledge, the limited degree of man's control of the world, the inevitability of death, the unalterable incidence of many forms of evil, the dangers accompanying progress and the constant proneness of man to follow the evil inclinations of his heart. The man who is forced to rely upon the messianic hope of self-deliverance cannot but be afraid of this limitation and has to denounce any allusion to it as retrograde. But where it is recognized and accepted in faith in the living God, it does not impede human activity, but helps towards respect for the freedom of man from tyranny and so towards respect for the mysteries of nature and history.

28. The acceptance of this limitation is of decisive importance at a time when instead of earlier forms of exploitation the individual is being absorbed more and more into the social system and his life is being organized more and more by social interests. Because Marxist doctrine in its form hitherto saw man only in his functional relation to society, but never admitted as valid that every man exists for his own sake, communism had no protection against the development of the struggle for liberty into new forms of slavery and the cynicism of officialdom; it fails to guard against the new forms of alienation resulting from technical and social progress. As against this the Christian stands for genuine liberty and the inviolability of every man, based on the fact that every man is the beloved child of God. He exists for his own sake, just as a lover is loved for himself alone and not for his position. By proclaiming the claim of

God's love to his creature, the Christian faith reveals the limit of law and the power of men and society over men and also over nature, and reveals God as man's protection against man.

29. Against the atheism imposed by the communist party Christianity is charged to witness to the reality of the living God. She is not charged to pronounce judgment on atheists. Neither with regard to men nor itself has Christianity to accept lightly the fact that today so many people flatly reject its witness, but at the same time it must not overlook the fact that—as Simone Weil said—there are two sorts of atheism, one of which is a clarification of the idea of God.

30. No matter to what depth refusal of the Christian faith may reach, even when it is a final rejection without any obvious reason, the Christian faith must meet it fundamentally with hope in the one who can soften stony hearts, cast out demons, heal the possessed and raise the dead. For this reason the Christian faith no longer thinks of the ice-cold of Marxist atheism as a last resort. It approaches it from the Cross, and so with penitence for its own guilt; and from Easter morning, and so with confidence that man's rejection of God is in the end powerless against God's will for man, to which the Christian bears witness in the world.

VIII

THE GOLLWITZER AFFAIR IN BASEL OR THE END OF FREEDOM

An Editorial in Junge Kirche made this comment, on 10th April 1962

THE PROTESTANT theological faculty of the University of Basel had been asked by the government to put forward only one name to fill the Chair of Systematic Theology vacated by Karl Barth. The choice of the Faculty was Professor Helmut Gollwitzer of Berlin. This proposal aroused a violent discussion in the Swiss press. The head of the department of education in the canton thereupon demanded that the faculty should increase the number of candidates so that a proper election could be held. The Faculty put forward several names, with Professor Gollwitzer's at the top of the list. At a meeting of the State Committee of Education the vote on the appointment of Professor Gollwitzer was inconclusive: four to four. The two Catholic members of the Committee had voted against Gollwitzer, but had abstained in the cases of the other candidates. So on the 19th of March the cantonal Minister of Education decided to veto Gollwitzer's appointment, without however deciding in favour of any one of the other candidates.

This extraordinary procedure can only be understood in the light of the knowledge of the background. It is obvious that Gollwitzer's rejection was the result of the political campaign of vilification that had been stirred up against him. This became particularly violent when Professor Gollwitzer wrote an article in the newspaper *Zürcher Woche* in defence of Professor Hromádka of Prague, who had been violently attacked in Switzerland. To help our readers to judge this dispute we are publishing the following:

1. An article by Professor Hromádka in the *Zürcher Woche*.
2. Professor Gollwitzer's comment on this.
3. An article by the Managing Editor of the *Basler Nachrichten*, Peter Dürrenmatt.
4. A comment from the *Zürcher Woche* with a letter from Professor Gollwitzer to Professor Lieb.[1]

Meanwhile it has become known that one of the remaining candidates, Dr Max Geiger, has withdrawn his candidature. The Basel Minister of Education has since then appointed the 33-year old Swiss theologian, Dr Heinrich Ott from Riehen near Basel to the vacant professorship. The West German newspaper *Die Welt* made this comment in its issue of April 4th: 'It was a political decision against the wishes of the Faculty and the student body, but in accord with the result of the referendum on the question of nuclear weapons. The Basel authorities would have liked to appoint Gollwitzer, the distinguished scholar and persuasive preacher, to the university chair, but not Gollwitzer the representative of the so-called "Movement for World Peace" and the spokesman of every anti-nuclear congress.'

Thus *Die Welt* confirms that in this case the so-called 'free West' has shown that even in the appointment to a chair of theology it is not the relevant qualifications that are decisive but political criteria derived from the cold war. *Die Zeit* wrote on the 6th of April: 'The government made this decision because it is critical of Gollwitzer's ambiguous attitude to communism. It is lamentable that even in one of the freest countries in the world a sincere attitude to God is no longer sufficient.'

[1]Nos. 3 and 4 are not translated for the purposes of this book.

IX

THE CHRISTIAN IN THE COMMUNIST SOCIETY

(*Zürcher Woche* No. 3, 19th January 1962)

Preface by the Zürcher Woche

DARE ONE risk allowing a prominent Christian from an eastern European state to express his views? We dare to do so, although those who do not appreciate our reasons will not be slow to criticize. If it is our duty as Christians to be concerned for the Christians in communist countries, we should not be afraid to listen to what they have to say. If we were no longer prepared to do this, we should be admitting that we are in the same position as any Czech paper, in which it is impossible for a western theologian to express his views. Professor Hromádka, Dean of the protestant Comenius Faculty in Prague, born in 1889, a former student of the University of Basel, gives in the following article his views on the position of a Christian in a communist state. He is expressing his own views, not those of the *Zürcher Woche*, let that be clearly understood. We have been careful to invite a western theologian, who himself knows at first hand through long experience conditions in eastern Europe, to write a comment on Professor Hromádka's article. Our readers will find Professor Helmut Gollwitzer's article on the following page. We hardly need to introduce the theologian Gollwitzer, the author of *Und führen wohin du nicht willst* (Eng. trans. *Unwilling Journey*)—Kaiser Verlag, Munich. The discussions about whether he should succeed Karl Barth in the professorship at Basel will also recall him to the Swiss public as a fearless Christian. All those who remember the visit of Professor Hromádka to the European regional conference of the World Protestant Alliance at Zürich in August 1961 will feel that the complementary articles by Hromádka and Gollwitzer are appropriate to a really free press.

Article by Dr Hromádka

In the discussions I have had about our attitude to the new socialist society I can pretty easily decide whether my vis-à-vis are concerned about the Christian faith or whether their interests and opinions are primarily political. So far I have not succeeded in convincing my fellow-Christians in the West that my main concern is for the truth of the Christian witness and the faithfulness of the Church of Jesus Christ. Whenever we are wrongly understood, we have to accept some of the blame and examine ourselves as to where and why we have failed to make our witness clear. It is however urgently necessary that our vis-à-vis or our opponents also give paramount importance to the heart of the Gospel and leave their own political interests aside, at least in the beginning of the discussion. If we disguise our political interests and convictions under a theological cloak, we shall be tempted to understand and interpret politically other people's theological statements or their attitude to the Church. Even nowadays, at the beginning of our discussions, there is an urgent need to understand each other about our ultimate motives and concern, to set ourselves in the searching light of the Gospel, so that we can talk to each other in mutual trust and know what are the ultimate issues at stake. In our human weakness we are never quite sure of ourselves. In particular we are seldom in a position to understand someone else completely and to see into the deepest motives of his heart. Nevertheless, it is our duty to strive with absolute honesty to understand ourselves and to interpret our vis-à-vis, even our most bitter opponent, as clearly as possible. We have not yet succeeded, I repeat, in achieving these prerequisites in our discussions. Herein lies the greatest defect in our internal ecumenical discussions, and it is our primary duty to overcome it. The differences in our attitude to and our understanding of the political and social situations in the world are not the most serious obstacle. They still exist of course and are part of the varied nature of the Christian community, but what is worse is the *a priori* mistrust and the temptation to judge and identify the other person according to our own prejudices.

For many years I have been involved in the theological controversies of modern times. All the burning questions concerning the reality and meaning of the divine self-revelation in the people of Israel, by the prophets and by the incarnation of the Word of God in Jesus of Nazareth, in his cross and resurrection, have been throughout the focal point of my theological work. And connected with this is the conflict over the existence and mission of the Church of Jesus Christ. We are in the middle of a total reconstruction of society in Central and Eastern Europe. What is at stake is not just a political change in the international situation, not just political reform in our countries, but the profound historical collapse of our civilization, our way of life and secular hopes for the future. The highest ideals and standards of western democracy have, in our view, ceased to be the norm, the standard and the arbiter of the future of man and of civilization. Unfortunately only a few people in the western churches have taken this seriously. They have also forgotten through what suffering, guilt and sin modern western civilization, with its wealth, its standard of living and its institutions, has reached its present dominance. And they have little understanding of the fact that the catastrophies of modern civilized mankind during the last half century have profoundly shattered their political aspirations and social structure, indeed even their ideological security. And we are not in a position to form any vivid picture of the millions of graves and the immense areas of devastated villages and towns, and to draw the right conclusions from this about the nature of the atmosphere in eastern Europe and across Siberia to the Pacific Ocean. I am personally convinced that western democracy, with its institutions, standards and culture, which failed in the critical years from 1918 to 1938, is unable to solve the problems of these areas. What was and is still necessary is a mighty effort and the readiness for sacrifices—of course with many failures, mistakes and shortcomings—to create a new stable social structure, a new beginning for these people, and to offer them new hope and a new incentive for more meaningful endeavour. Is it conceivable that the Church with its institutions, customs, way of life, traditional moral and ideological outlook, should not be shaken? The anti-religious and anti-clerical attitude of the present architects of the new social-political cultural structure is in part the legacy of the western intellectual position, in part a political attack on all the old pillars of a society to be conquered.

In this situation we find ourselves witnesses to the Gospel and responsible members of our ancient historic Church. This situation must not be assessed from a party-political standpoint, or according to traditional principles assumed as self-evident, or even according to the prejudices of western European or American bourgeoisie. On our side there is no anti-western feeling. I am personally deeply rooted in the true dynamic of western thought. But our situation far transcends the limits of the party-politics of a parochial European system or of a self-assured American system. We are standing literally amid the ruins of what even half a century ago was regarded as the highest ideal of European democracy. I remember T. G. Masaryk, Woodrow Wilson and others. We are shocked by the ossification of the liberal-bourgeois as well as the social-democratic parties, and we wonder frankly and after much self-examination what would happen if the soviet and socialist countries of eastern Europe and Asia should collapse and the way to the East were opened to the western nations. The outcome would be almost beyond imagination.

It is against this background that our western fellow-Christians, and above all the western nations, should understand us. It should be remembered that our struggle is an organic extension of our theological work and tensions, of our, I hope, honest devotion to the heart of the Gospel, our longing for perfect freedom in the presence of the risen and victorious Jesus, for the freedom which is the unconditional prerequisite of a clear understanding of the actual situation and of a courageous witness among present-day working, creating, sceptical, half-believing and unbelieving people, but is also the prerequisite of a loving and compassionate understanding of those who are carrying on their shoulders an enormous and almost unbearable burden of responsibility. I am continually worried and almost shocked, when I hear the stereotyped, abstract and indiscriminate words about 'the free world', and 'totalitarian tyranny', about Christianity and atheism or about an atheistic state, and indeed when we find our path obstructed by all the forms of demonology in which western man goes on living. The spiritual conflict in which we are involved is beyond our strength, and our strength is weakened and our efforts hampered when people try obstinately to convince us that every attempt at Christian witness in the new socialist or communist society is either a feeble compromise, dishonest opportunism, or even treachery to the cause of Jesus Christ. We find ourselves between the two millstones: on the one hand we are continually hearing from representatives of the official ideology that in the new society the Christian faith and the Church will gradually die out, thanks to the irresistible progress of science and technology and the final elimination of all social weaknesses, and, on the other hand, we hear from the West words like 'opportunism', and 'betrayal'. As a result our struggle is impeded and made more difficult. In all humility I would say, however, that we do not give up, that we do not allow ourselves to be discouraged, but that we are on the contrary spurred on to love our fellow citizens the more ardently, whether believers or unbelievers, to sustain them in our own way in their efforts at reconstruction, to examine ourselves as to whether we have sufficient strength and whether we ourselves believe wholeheartedly in the Gospel and are following our Lord Jesus faithfully, and whether we are able to appease the spiritual hunger that will sooner or later reappear. For our part we should like to ask our fellow Christians, who fail to understand us, the simple question whether they are really sure of their faith or not, whether the spiritual situation in the western countries is so obviously better than it is with us, and whether it is really possible to work successfully for the Gospel in a bourgeois capitalist country. I must not over-simplify our situation. Christianity, or rather belief in the Gospel and the Church of Jesus Christ, is not taken for granted here any longer. We bear in addition to our own sins the sins and shortcomings of our fathers and forefathers. Indeed we bear on our shoulders also the sins and weaknesses of western Christians and their attacks upon us, all the attempts to undermine the socialist world and even to bring about its downfall, in the name of Christianity and of the Christian Church. Here I would not only defend myself, but venture upon a modest riposte. The manner in which the socialist countries and communism are treated in the name of Christianity is fundamentally wrong, perverse and likely to be the grave-digger of the Church in many lands, not only in the East.

I hope my readers will not misunderstand me. I do not want to give the impression that as a Christian I am identifying myself with the present socialist structure or trying to make propaganda for socialism or even communism. For one thing, as a Christian my understanding extends beyond the limits of what the new social structure can do for men. Although I am convinced that through the new political and social order people are being helped more efficiently and permanently in many respects, particularly materially, but also culturally and morally, yet I know very well that human dignity and fulfilment cannot be achieved or ensured by any social, economic or cultural order. However perfect the external organization may be, it does not deal with the realities of life and death, guilt and forgiveness, friendship and love, loyalty and readiness for sacrifice. It is our supreme task to strive for and on behalf of the men who are on the threshold of the new order and who will be living in the socialistically planned and furnished edifice. We do not believe that the way of life produced by mere social, political, economic and technical progress can satisfy the ultimate desires of men and remain their only hope. The nature, mystery and mission of man are so high and deep that no social order and no civilization, however rich, can realize them and assure them and overcome our sense of guilt. Furthermore, it must be insisted that the Gospel and the living Church of Jesus Christ are not dependent on any external order, and that they ride on majestically across the ruins of the old social order and civilization and give to the man on the threshold of a new social and political experiment all the courage, freedom and love necessary for a new beginning. I reject all the whispered suggestions, from whichever side they come, that in the new society being created under a secular or anti-clerical ideology the Gospel cannot be preached and that the Church must inevitably perish. The Lord, in whom we believe, is Lord also of the new order and of the future. In his name we must bear before unbelievers genuine witness to the truth of Jesus of Nazareth, and in true penitence, but with great courage and love, make a way into the community of believers for the masses who have been estranged from the Church through our guilt and that of our fathers. If we perish, it will be because of our guilt, disobedience and hardness of heart. How tremendous our task is! How deep must our faith be and our devotion and our courage to love! Is there any greater need today than to strive for each other, to encourage and love each other, instead of correcting and judging each other peevishly and with suspicion?

X

SHARING THE LOT OF CHRISTIANS IN THE EASTERN STATES

by Helmut Gollwitzer in response to Josef Hromádka

Preface by the Zürcher Woche

We made Professor Hromádka's manuscript available to his colleague, Professor Helmut Gollwitzer, and asked him to write a reply or a critique. Professor Gollwitzer, who is staying for some time in Switzerland, wrote to us recently: 'Here is what you asked for, but I do not know whether it is what you wanted. You asked for a reply to Hromádka and that I have not produced, because I find myself in considerable agreement with his article. I might suggest a few critical questions about one or two of his remarks on the situation in the western democracies, but that seemed to me inopportune, as possibly weakening the essential impact on western readers of Hromádka's burning words. And so I have written only an apologia, or rather an attempt to facilitate understanding, instead of a reply.'

In these circumstances the debate is still open. Our readers, particularly the theologians among them, are invited to comment on both Hromádka's article and Gollwitzer's reply.

Article by Dr Gollwitzer

The foregoing article from Professor Hromádka, the important theologian in Prague, is one of the most moving appeals that have reached us so far from the countries behind the so-called iron curtain. It is a plea that we in the West—contrary to what we usually do—should try to share in the lot and the problems of the people in the eastern states. It is a plea for fellow feeling, which is regarded as more important than all other forms of assistance, material, financial, political or even military. It is often loudly complained that it is not possible for us to help the people over there in these various ways, so we should be all the more interested in a request for something entirely within our power and which perhaps we had not thought of before.

What is Hromádka asking for? That we should share their thinking, that our sympathy with the oppressed and indignation against the oppressors should be transformed into a responsible attempt at understanding with particular reference to the Christians in communist countries, and since our sympathy is mainly centred on them and their fate made familiar to the western public, the position of Christians over there may be taken as an example. Prayers have been offered for them in western churches since 1917. But is any attempt being made to share their thinking? That would entail trying to know their real situation, to keep abreast of the development of their actual conditions, to examine critically the information put out in the propaganda war, if possible by personal visits and contacts, and above all trying as far as possible to put ourselves in their position and to think out the questions that face them every day. These questions do not concern only the persecution and restrictions to which Christians in those countries are often exposed, or the courage needed for a defiant confession, or the arguments against atheism. The much more serious questions relate to the tasks facing a Christian in his Christian life in this changed world.

Anyone who visits these countries and talks to serious Christians living there discovers to his surprise how glad they are when their western visitor shows an interest in these tasks and discusses them without prejudice. We tend to see only the task of resistance to communism. Probably our own egoism plays a part in this. In the conflict with communism we want the non-communists in the eastern countries, and especially the Christians, as our allies, as cells of resistance, as fifth columnists, as potential counter-revolutionaries. We meet them with self-evident expectation and if they do not fulfil it they either cease to interest us or they are suspect as Quislings and collaborators. In all this we hardly consider that in this way we are confirming the communist assumption of the close connection between Christianity and capitalism, and are providing the communists with an argument justifying their treatment of the Church and indeed inciting them to advocate the destruction of the Church. A distinguished Catholic authority on Marxism said a short time ago that many Christians in the West seem to share the conviction of Stalinists in the East that as many bishops as possible should be imprisoned by the communists. That is how it is, in fact, as long as we think in a cliché of resistance and demand of the Christians in the East, that all they have to do is to fulfil this our expectation of them—not to mention the fact that here in the West many people speak and write in this way who so far have given no evidence in their own lives that, faced with the same test, they would not be guilty of the very opportunism and collaborationism of which they glibly accuse men like Hromádka.

Josef L. Hromádka became widely known outside Czechoslovakia through the letter sent to him by Karl Barth in 1938 supporting him and his Czech fellow Christians in their resistance to Hitler. Today he is condemned by the West because he is not carrying on the same sort of resistance to the present government, either openly or underground. But it should, of course, be clearly realized that here we are not dealing with just a nobody, who happens to have been thrown up by the hazard of events. Since the early 'twenties, as a Professor in the theological faculty of the small evangelical minority Church, Hromádka has been its most powerful spiritual exponent, and for many years the teacher and spiritual father of its clergy, a man of high intellectual culture, uniting in his thought the inspiration of Masaryk's philosophy and Barth's theology. He is an incontestably trustworthy Christian, upheld by the confidence of his Church. This Church is an extremely live community, though small, that has had to endure persecution since the days of its first martyr Johannes Hus and the counter-reformation. It has splendid young ministers and live congregations. I have met many people there who do not agree with Hromádka's rather optimistic view of the future development of communism and of the advantages of the socialist organization, but none who, in spite of their differences, have not the most complete trust in him as a Christian or have any doubt of his integrity or that all his words and actions are prompted by his Christian faith. That is a rare phenomenon in an atmosphere of widespread suspicion.

Of all the noteworthy representatives of the Christian Church in the East Hromádka is the one who has thought out most intensively, frankly and boldly—always in the light of the Christian faith—the character of the new situation and the consequent tasks of Christians and the Christian congregations in a world dominated by communism. He therefore commands increasing attention far beyond his own community, from Protestant, Catholic and Orthodox Churches in a similar situation. The incompatibility of communist atheism and Christianity is as obvious to him as to the communists, but that does not exhaust the implications of the Christian life in the communist state. Being a Christian is not mere negation. It means sharing responsibility with others, wherever God has placed us. Besides the task of resistance, i.e. the public confession of the Christian faith over against atheism, the Christian has the equally important task of working responsibly as a member of society. Among the texts often quoted in discussions about the role of Christians in the eastern countries, the exhortation of the Prophet Jeremiah to the exiled Jews in Babylon is particularly apt: 'Seek the peace of the city.' This means seeking the best for that society, which one has not chosen and by which one is treated with hostility on account of one's beliefs. The particular exhortation that Hromádka addressed to the people and especially the Christians overwhelmed by communism can thus be summarized:

1. This is no passing misfortune but an irrevocable change. Therefore do not keep dreaming of a return to the past: do not

try to hibernate; do not hope for liberation by the West—but look forwards!

2. The forward-looking hope must not be directed towards the collapse of the communist régime, which could only come about through war with its immeasurable chaos and without any certainty of improvement, but should look to the divine Lord of History, who can bring about transformations and create possibilities beyond what we in our godless resignation can imagine. Therefore do not paint a static negative picture and stare at that, but distinguish between the negative and positive possibilities, decide where one can go along with the rest and where not. Do not overlook any positive tendencies, but assist them. Join with those communists who are seriously concerned about the humane aims of communism and about the welfare of the people in its power—and there are such everywhere! Do not preserve a negative attitude of bitter hostility to the communist system, but contribute to the task of making it something that can be discussed in human terms.

3. The Christian's conflict with communist atheism must not be fought on a political level, not openly or secretly as a factor in the struggle between West and East, but it must be fought without any political alignment, hope and ulterior purpose, as a struggle for the soul of the atheists. What is at stake is not liberation from communism in the personal interests of the individual, but the liberation of the communists from the dogmatic insistence on atheism, which mars their aims. This can only come about if the Christians at least become penitent and believe, i.e. recognize communism as a judgment on the unchristlikeness of the Christians and the Christian Church and the so-called Christian nations and the policy exercised by them. It means at the same time maintaining a genuine faith in the conquering power of the Gospel, to which they so often give lip service.

A well known Swiss journalist wrote a little while ago that it was a complete delusion to imagine that Christians in the eastern countries could exert any responsible influence on the developments there: they were in fact condemned to impotence and had only the choice between becoming puppets or martyrs. But it is precisely the liberation from the acceptance of this pattern of thought that is the important thing for the people over there. This pattern degrades men by reducing them either to cynical opportunists or fanatics. The Christian over there cannot of course exercise influence by the methods of our parliamentary democracy, nor have they the power to change the régime, but they are not thereby absolved from a share in the responsibility for the progress of their people and their society. To deny them this is to deny their humanity and their position as Christians. To call them to this task is to remind them that they still have far more possibilities than they at first thought in their bitterness and despair. That is confirmed by countless individual local and regional experiences. The process of liberalization in the East, of which we have such clear evidence today, did not fall from heaven, but is due to many factors, among which the continual insistence on human responsibility on the part of many communists and Christians is an essential though not the only one.

To us in the West this means that we do not need to suppress our anxious and critical questions in face of those statements by eastern Christians which sound suspiciously like conformity. On the contrary by our questioning we must share their really difficult burden. But only those can ask questions helpfully who do not make demands from their high horse and their comfortable western armchairs, or urge western clichés upon them, but try to place themselves in their position, in their daily conflict with communist demands on Christianity, for which there is after all material enough in their Christian and national share of responsibility. And above all questions can be most helpfully asked by those who are willing to face their questions, and those who see and resist the danger of conformity, of misuse of Christianity for most unchristian interests, of opportunism and forced opinions, not only on the opposite side but also on our own—in the spirit of the picture in the Sermon on the Mount of the mote and the beam.

By taking part in this way in the problems of the people and the Christians in the East we can help them in their test of constancy, in which they are involved, and will gain not a little for our own problems.

XI

CASTING OUT DEMONS

A Sermon at the reopening of the restored church of St John at Berlin-Schlachtensee, 31st July, 1960

The memorial plaque bears the inscription

LORD THOU HAST CHASTENED US
1914—1939
The fallen, those killed by bombs,
Those destroyed as being unworthy to live,
Those sacrificed in resistance,
The murdered Jews, the Martyrs for their faith,
The missing, the deported, the despairing—
The blood of them all cries to thee.
Lord, have mercy on our distress and guilt,
Make us messengers of thy peace.

The text was taken from St Mark 5.1-20.

MY DEAR friends, what is the purpose of the services held in this church, this newly restored building, to which we are returning today? What is the meaning of these bells ringing out so challengingly, so urgently, so loudly, across the town? The answer is: There are demons to be cast out by the power of God! Nothing less! There are slaves to be freed, heavy iron chains that must fall, prison walls that must be broken down, so that men who have long been shut away from daylight may stagger forth from their dark captivity still weak and uncertain, still bearing deep lacerations caused by their fetters. This strange story of that unfortunate man is not just a remarkable incident from the distant past: it proclaims what shall happen today, and why we are gathered here. We have not come to listen to eloquent sermons: to ring the bells to invite people here for that would be truly presumptuous. We have not come in order to cosset our own religious sensibilities and to cultivate our own religious emotional life: reading poetry or listening to music would be useful for that. We come together to listen to stories like this, and as we listen to be brought under the same divine power, and so that the story of this unfortunate man may be our story, mine and yours. Indeed the beginning of the story is our story. May its end be our story, too!

In this demoniac the listener is shown a picture of himself. Surely that cannot be! I am not at all like that! On the one side of the picture we have the respectable citizens of Gadara, with their fields and herds of pigs—or perhaps the solid citizens of Schlachtensee, the officials and tradesmen and professors and the dear old people in their old folks' homes, with their gardens. On the other side of the picture we see this horrible raving lunatic, dangerous and shameless. There is all the difference in the world! That was the reason why he had been driven out into isolation from the society of sane respectable and acceptable people. We in Germany have long believed in this distinction and have regarded the demon stories of the New Testament as old tales handed down from a barbarous age. Culture and education, so we thought, had banished the fear of demons and taught us to distinguish our noble humanity from horrible aberrations and distortions of human nature like those so often given prominence in the New Testament. They are regrettable exceptions that must be banished out of sight—but the New Testament brings them back into view: it keeps putting Jesus alongside these 'exceptions', and shows them being drawn to him as though with a magnet. The New Testament says clearly: If you want to understand the human situation you must not be deceived by the façade of culture, the veneer of education, the humanist whitewash. You must not shrink from looking at this horrible picture of humanity out there among the tombs. To understand you must look just where God looks, as he decides to become man in order to save men. 'To be unable to endure the truth about men—that is idealism' (Nietzsche). And God is not an idealist nor is the Bible an idealistic book. The truth about man was made horribly clear when the nations that were in the van of human progress, the bearers of all the noble fruits of the human spirit, attacked each other in the twentieth century with every conceivable kind of savagery. The truth about man, not as he should be, not as God created him, but as he is now in his strange dereliction, is inscribed on the memorial tablet that we are unveiling in this church today.

> The fallen, those killed by bombs,
> Those destroyed as being unworthy to live,
> Those sacrificed in resistance,
> The murdered Jews, the martyrs for their faith,
> The missing, the deported, the despairing—

That is the measure of the savage fury with which men have fought against men. They have heard the Gospel, they have read Goethe and Schiller at school, they have enjoyed the music of Mozart, they have probed the mysteries of nature in the interests of science—and then this! Horrors so frightful and outrageous that we cannot bear even to hear about them, and many of you push away out of sight the books about concentration camps, as the only way to ensure a night's sleep. Who would have thought that this sort of thing was latent in a nation like ours, that our respectable citizens—not born criminals, but worthy fathers of families—were capable of such atrocities? We cannot even say that this was just a passing aberration that we have left behind us, for what else is the meaning of the frightful preparations for war with which the peoples of the world are facing each other again today, after such horrors, from which they have learned nothing, if it is not the desperate threat: if you over there touch our possessions and rights, then we will repeat in greater measure all the horrors of the last world war, and spare neither women nor children nor the unborn infants of future generations. As the angels in heaven look down on these men of the twentieth century, can they form any other picture of them than that of the raving demoniac of Gadara, driven to and fro by evil spirits, uncontrollable and dangerous, destroying themselves and everything around them? What else can they do at this sight up there before the throne of God, or we down here amongst the war graves, but cry: 'O God, look down from heaven and have mercy!'? And this is all the more true, since the demons do not only work their mischief amongst the nations, but they do the same in individual lives. And we in this congregation also, in the privacy of our homes, behind the neat rough-cast exterior and the tidy gardens, in our domestic life and in the office and in our inmost individual hearts, struggle against our chains, and contrary to all common sense, good advice and good resolutions, are powerless against bondage to our impulses, against fear, cowardice, unrestrained ambition, against contempt and disregard for our fellows and the poisoning of our social life, can only cry: 'O God, look down from heaven and have mercy on us!'

That is the beginning of the story. Then the picture of human helplessness changes—for it is not only the demoniac who is helpless, but also those who have driven him out—as Jesus comes in. Jesus lands on the shore of helplessness and comes into the land of demons. The demoniac rushes at him with superhuman strength in order to kill him or drive him away—and see! Jesus does not run away like all the others, but the demoniac falls on his knees before him. And all the rest of the story—this strange conversation between Jesus and the demons, whose name is legion, this cringing of the dreaded demons, this pleading to be allowed a dwelling place at least in the despised pigs that were considered unclean—all this only makes clear how completely the situation changed with the appearance of Jesus, and that the power is now on the other side. We have been looking about us in bewilderment. No power seemed sufficient to cope with the force that had bound the spirit of man in chains. God was a long way off in his heaven and we were alone down here. This story is set in a heathen land, with its demon-infested life, so like the twentieth century, and in the heathen land the word is spoken: 'Be gone, you dismal spirits, for the Lord of Joy, Jesus Christ, is here!' And so the story goes further—against other evil spirits, that in face of the truth about man try to enslave our spirit—against the spirit of loneliness, of despair, of 'nothing is any use', of surrender and resignation. The story is not intended as portraying an isolated event, but is a call from disciples who have known this experience themselves and who point us to Jesus present among us, and run before him crying: 'Have courage, you slaves, your deliverer is coming. Run to meet him, offer your fettered hearts and hands to him, trust him for the help no other can give! It is not true that there is no helper anywhere: it is not true that your fate is to be possessed by demons: it is not true that God is dead or far off in his heaven. He is not far, but is here among you and is ready and willing to hear the cry of the needy!' Every story in the Bible is a promise of freedom: every time it speaks of God it is not pointing up into a far-away heaven, but to the Lord of creation coming down here to us in our land of demons, seeking men and ready and able to save, restore and set men free. Every service is a call to discipleship, the proclamation of the mighty Saviour, the coming of the word that robs the demons of their power. Every service is a challenge to us not to believe any more in the power of demons, however great it seems, but to believe in the Saviour who in simple unpretentious human guise goes forth against the evil power of the whole legion of demons. We belong to him and not to them. That is the meaning of our baptism, repeated in every communion service:

Satan, I tell you this:
I am a baptized Christian.
So I can defeat you,
However terrible you are.
When I came here for baptism,
All your power was taken from you
And God's covenant frees me
From your tyranny.

That is what the story says: that is what every service says, and its truth is not affected by whatever questions we attempt to bring forward. Why does God let these evil spirits work their mischief at all? Why did the poor man have to suffer so long? Why did not God through Jesus wipe out all the demons at once? Why are there only occasional isolated manifestations of his power? On that the story, and indeed the whole Bible, remains silent: it leaves such questions until the day when in the fuller light of heaven we shall understand God's reasons and adore his wisdom. He just says to us: Help is here! So we have the simple choice either to let ourselves be submerged by all these questions and to surrender to the power of evil, or to cling to his hand and let him lead us and not to let go even when we are not completely and finally rescued at the first pull, but for a while move backwards and forwards between freedom and bondage. When Jesus set this demoniac free the news sent out a ray of hope for all the afflicted, for all in bondage, in the country round about. The hope that his news kindled in them was the first stretching out of the Saviour's hand towards them, the first germ of a new life. At that moment they ceased to be completely enslaved. They were already beginning to rebel against the evil power. They were no longer supine and without the will-power or the means to escape. And this news is ready to do the same for us: first a hope, then a cry for help, and soon a stirring of revolt against slavery and a movement towards freedom, and that brings about the inflowing of new power, and we go back again and again to the places where others who have heard this news come together in the presence of the Saviour himself and receive power for their daily struggle of freedom against bondage. We shall have wonderful experiences of liberation in our lives, and we shall find new hope for those times when we are struggling desperately in the net laid for us by evil spirits. The hope shining from this news has the power to prevent us from falling or giving up. This memorial tablet too reminds us of this and of the liberating power of the Holy Spirit. It reminds us not only of the night and the horror, but of the light of hope shining through the darkness. Along with all the talk of the sacrifices of those days that we have so often heard, there are many words that tell of a great sense of freedom, written in death cells with manacled hands, in a hopeless situation that seemed the complete antithesis of freedom. How is it possible for us to have so forgotten our standards? Outward freedom is a great boon—that we have today—but are we really free? Are not the spirits of destruction still carrying on their work of mischief in a more subtle form? Can we really afford to go running hither and thither seeking all sorts of panaceas, while this freedom-giving power has not done its work in us?

It is remarkable, as our story indicates, how differently the actions of Jesus can be received. One man wanted to stay with Jesus and the others wanted to get rid of him. There are spirits that quite obviously would destroy our lives, and we welcome joyfully someone who can deliver us from them. But there are other spirits in servitude to whom we feel comfortable, and for that reason Jesus has more difficulty with the supposedly healthy than with the sick, more difficulty with the righteous than with the publicans and sinners. Those farmers who are angry with him because of the loss of their pigs and consider a man of less value than a herd of swine are a greater problem than the legion of devils in the sick man. The demons of money, prosperity, material, intellectual, moral and religious possessions, enslave men more surely and more subtly. Then Jesus seems sinister, freedom seems sinister, and the divine spirit seems dangerous, that gives us joy in poverty and insecurity, and courage for all the great and small experiences of life and joy in every man who is restored, even when it costs us suffering and sacrifice. Which of the two pictures is really sadder, the beginning of the story with the bleeding, screaming maniac amongst the tombs, or the end, with these ordinary, normal men who have come out to see Jesus and beside him the man he has cured talking sanely and confidentially to him? Instead of cheering for joy at this marvellous sight, these men have no eyes for anything but their sows and their money! What good are the deeds of God to us, however wonderful, if our hearts are not free for joy and gratitude, like the heart of this sick man who was healed? Jesus taught them a great lesson: a man is more important than any possessions, so do not grieve for your herd of swine, but rejoice over this man who has been restored into the image of God. How much was a man worth in the old days of slavery? What is he worth now in the twentieth century in a period of over-population? How many men have been sacrificed and impoverished for money or for honour? How many hundreds of thousands have been sacrificed for national power, for pride of race, for the madness of politicians? Now we are ready to sacrifice millions more for the sake of the western or eastern way of life, and there sits Jesus and the man he healed, and Jesus says to him: 'Go and tell the others. Go and help your friends by telling them what great things the merciful Lord has done for you!' That means tell them that the eternal God cares for men, that to him every individual is of infinite value. The idols that men worship are merciless tyrants, continually demanding of us human sacrifices. But the man who finds the freedom that Jesus gives is free to sacrifice himself for others, but he cannot take part in sacrificing men for ideas or political aims and all sorts of idols. When the Vichy government handed over to Hitler the French Jews to be murdered in order to save the rest of France, the French poet Bernanos wrote: 'We must not countenance that, we must not be willing to rebuild the life of France on the life of even one innocent Jewish child.' In addition to the guilt which we too share, particularly as a Christian congregation with this memorial tablet before us, there is the further fact that we have again and again condoned this evil design. Many of us thought that we had to accept the murder of the Jews and the feeble-minded, so long as we won the war. The Church has not taken seriously enough nor emphasized what is after all written here in the New Testament: Man is of more value than things. In Jesus God becomes the brother of man. The life of the least among his brethren is precious in his sight. The Church of Jesus Christ only lives in freedom when it no longer takes part in sacrificing men on the altars of idols, when it opposes this oppression and exploitation and degrading of men, when it opposes hot wars and cold wars, in which men are regarded not as men but as enemies, as human material. The call of the Synod of Eisenach in 1948 was 'Look at man!' and today there is no less cause to repeat that call in East and West alike. Bishops, generals and statesmen may refuse penitence. This memorial tablet calls us, the survivers, to penitence, and asks us in regard to our private and public life: What are you doing to your brother? Are you letting him be put to the sword for you, or have you been set free by the words you have heard here, free to serve your neighbour, free from fear for your own life, so that you can help care for the life of your neighbour? We see Jesus sitting beside our brother whom we have driven out because of his evil spirit. We see only the evil in him. But now we must see what Jesus does, see him sitting beside Jesus healed, and seeing this become messengers of healing for him. It is to prepare us for this that we have been given this house of God and its services. Amen.

INDEX